CHRIST · CHURCH · MANKIND

The Spirit of
Vatican II according to
POPE JOHN PAUL II

Edited by Zdzisław Józef Kijas, OFM Conv,
and Andrzej Dobrzyński

Paulist Press
New York / Mahwah, NJ

Front cover photo credits: Large photo, top, courtesy of Denis Babenko/Shutterstock.com. Small photos at bottom, from left to right: (1), (2), and (3) courtesy of the archives of the Archdiocese of Krakow; (4) and (5) courtesy of Nikodem Powojski, OFM Conv.

Cover and book design by Sharyn Banks

This title was first published as *Cristo–Chiesa–Uomo: Il Vaticano II nel Pontificato di Giovanni Paulo II*. Copyright © 2011 by Libreria Editrice Vaticana, Sede Centrale: Via della Posta s/n–00120 Città del Vaticano

English translation by Sean O'Neill. Copyright © 2012 by Paulist Press, Inc.

Library of Congress Cataloging-in-Publication Data

International symposium on "Vatican II in the Pontificate of John Paul II" (2008 : Rome, Italy)
    Christ, church, mankind : the spirit of Vatican II according to Pope John Paul II / edited by Zdzisław Józef Kijas and Andrzej Dobrzyński; translated by Sean O'Neill.
    p. cm.
    Includes bibliographical references and index.
    ISBN 978-0-8091-4762-5 (alk. paper)
    1. John Paul II, Pope, 1920–2005—Congresses. 2. Vatican Council (2nd : 1962–1965)—Congresses. 3. Theology, Doctrinal—History—20th century—Congresses. I. Kijas, Zdzisław Józef. II. Dobrzyński, Andrzej, 1968- III. Pontificia facoltà teologica "S. Bonaventura" (Rome, Italy) IV. Centro di documentazione e studio sul pontificato di Giovanni Paolo II. V. Title.
    BX1378.5.C66713 2008
    282.09´0511—dc23

2012006009

Published by Paulist Press
997 Macarthur Boulevard
Mahwah, New Jersey 07430

www.paulistpress.com

Printed and bound in the
United States of America

CONTENTS

OPENING STATEMENT

CARDINAL STANISLAW RYŁKO
*President of the Pontifical Council for the Laity
and of the John Paul II Foundation*

"Christ, Church, Mankind..." These are the subjects we wish to examine in the context of this international assembly on "Vatican II in the Pontificate of John Paul II," which was organized by the St. Bonaventure-Seraphicum Pontifical Theology Faculty and by the Center for the Documentation and Study of the Pontificate of John Paul II, which is part of the John Paul II Foundation. Exactly thirty years from the election of Cardinal Wojtyła to the Chair of Peter, we feel the need to reflect on the key themes of the Council and of the pontificate of John Paul II. His pontificate, from 1978 to 2005, focused specifically on those key themes, as the pontiff repeatedly emphasized. In the light of modern culture and of the challenge that it poses to humanity, to the Church, and to the world at large, it seems particularly important to stop and reflect on these key issues.

We often experience past times, just as our modern times, as very dark on the cultural, spiritual, and religious level. These are times in which we particularly recognize the power of certain human and spiritual values that are fundamental for the life of mankind, at least in contrast to the times. It is thus that the themes of the Council, which were so dear to the Holy Father John Paul II, emerge now, even more than in the past, as fundamental to the human community's rediscovering itself and its sense of purpose.

Nighttime, with the silence and the quiet that fill its time and space, is often the best time to go over the events of the day, process them, contemplate them, and draw from them useful teachings for life as it goes on. So our modern times, which seem to be somewhat

v

lacking in incisive values and marked by a certain "silence" about what matters, by a kind of night, can be a good point at which to look again at the richness of the recent past, to consider it again in the light of the reality of our present day, and to take from it the strength needed for us to continue to shape history, a history that continues and in which the precious lives of the men and women of our time play out.

In Krakow on July 16, 1962, Karol Wojtyła was named vicar-general of the Archdiocese of Krakow and participated in the work of the Council in this capacity. Providence allowed him to partici-pate in all the sessions of the Council, with mind and heart attentive to the movements of the Spirit that guided those meetings, which were intense, sometimes conflicted, but very, very fruitful for the life of humanity in the following years. Witnesses describe him as busy listening and at the same time writing what was probably a re-working—albeit personal—of the riches that emerged from those sessions. During that time he was taking notes for his future text on the renewal of the Council, later published under the title *Sources of Renewal*, the firstfruits, in his mind, of an experience that would leave its mark on the whole of his existence.

A true contemplative as he had always been, Bishop Wojtyła ex-amined the work of God as well as the words and the meetings that he encountered in Rome, while he celebrated with the Church that historic Council. In keeping with his philosophical background and with the Slavic personalism that particularly marked his thought and his perspective of faith, his contribution is expressed in the drafting of *Gaudium et Spes*, the Council's pastoral constitution that deals with announcing the faith in the modern world. The delicate and pro-found attention to the problems and tensions of humanity in this time—and even beyond our own era—stimulated him and the other members of the responsible committee to work out a true and proper spiritual and human vision of history worthy of the Gospel, which is the announcement that Christ is the Son of God, made true man for us and among us, made our contemporary, and is in search of men and women in their own time.

The young auxiliary bishop of Krakow saw in the Council, even then, what immediately took root in the depths of his soul and mo-tivated his choices. When he returned to his homeland, he called a

Synod of the Church in Krakow (1972–79). He fully understood the truth about the Church and the people of God, a people composed of brothers and sisters in whom there are different roles but in whom there is also equal dignity. He immediately wanted to make the Church that he belonged to aware of the conciliar vision, above all allowing the Church to live the new and full dimensions of dialog and shared commitment that the ecclesial event had opened up.

In 1978, the archbishop of Krakow was elected pope, to his surprise. His ease in relating to everyone immediately opened lines of communication that made them understand that the Church wished to approach the men and women of its time.

Looking back at the teaching of this great pope and his style of being pastor of the Universal Church, we can rediscover the three fixed points of the Council: Christ, the Church, and mankind. In reality, they were not three distinct points of his message, but three aspects of the same word. We could say, rather, three loves, encompassed in the one great love of his existence: God, the only one to love, serve, and announce by every means possible.

To turn to Christ, to know him as the only-begotten Son of God, meant for Pope John Paul II to find truth in the Church, Christ's mystical body, recognizing in him the light that shines on his face and the truth about mankind, which, as *Gaudium et Spes* says, finds itself only in Christ.

This is expressed from the beginning in the encyclical *Redemptor Hominis* but is confirmed often in other subsequent documents, such as the *Catechism*. It is sufficient to recall the catechetical notes on human love of the 1980s to rediscover a refined symphony of these three arias: Christ, who founds his Church and encounters mankind in every time to announce to us our dignity as sons and daughters, and brothers and sisters to all.

The ardent passion for Jesus Christ spurred the pope to find every method of carrying the good news and the presence of the Church to all people, in every corner of the Earth, in his many apostolic travels and in the numerous personal meetings that marked the days of the long, almost twenty-seven years of his pontificate. The same passions gave life to his desire to speak to all manner of persons, believers or not, without ever admitting exceptions to the integrity of the Gospel message, but ready to discover even unforeseen ways to make it understandable for anyone who might be far from encountering the only Savior.

The historical era in which John Paul II lived and exercised the delicate Petrine ministry was a complex time, rife with tensions with which he willingly engaged in his own flesh, from the terrible attempt on his life in 1981 to the last days of his existence. Revisiting this long period, which this international assembly has made possible, has helped us, however, to understand better that Christ and his Church are alive in every historical era, even the most difficult ones, and that their only concern is mankind, seeking out every man and every woman where they live, suffer, and rejoice. They only wish to announce to them that Love is alive and is with us, that justice is possible with Christ and we must seek it out, and that the truth makes us free and gives us dignity.

This is how the themes of Christ, Church, and mankind take on concrete significance and become the history of humanity even in our time. This is how, through John Paul II, what the Holy Council Fathers lived and worked out during the sessions of Vatican II becomes an opportunity for modern men and women for renewed freedom, for authentic happiness, for equilibrium between *nova et vetera*. This equilibrium never forgets its Gospel roots, the witness of tradition, but desires to make it alive today, incisive in our time, perhaps a time that is obscure and contradictory, but still the time of Christ, the time of the Church, the favorable time to be truly men and women according to God's plan.

THE SIGNIFICANCE OF THE COUNCIL

We can affirm that the Second Vatican Council was a providential event, whereby the Church began the more immediate preparation for the Jubilee of the Second Millennium. It was a Council similar to earlier ones, yet very different; it was a Council focused on the mystery of Christ and his Church and at the same time open to the world. This openness was an evangelical response to recent changes in the world, including the profoundly disturbing experiences of the twentieth century, a century scarred by the First and Second World Wars, by the experience of concentration camps, and by horrendous massacres. All these events demonstrate most vividly that the world needs purification; it needs to be converted.

JOHN PAUL II, *Tertio Millennio Adveniente*, n. 18

"LET US SPEAK TO MANKIND IN AN INTELLIGIBLE WAY..."

HIS EMINENCE CARDINAL TARCISIO BERTONE
Secretary of the Vatican State

My Lord Cardinals,

Dear Brother Bishops and Priests,

Reverend Father Rector and Faculty at the Seraphicum,

Dear Students,

Ladies and Gentlemen,

It is with great pleasure that I address you at the beginning of this International Study Convention whose theme is "Christ, Church, Mankind: Vatican II in the Pontificate of John Paul II." On October 16 last, on the exact day and hour thirty years ago when Cardinal Karol Wojtyła was elected pontiff, the film *Witness* was shown in the presence of the pope. It is an account that retraced the experiences, both human and spiritual, of John Paul II, narrated by his faithful personal secretary, Father Stanislaus, now Archbishop of Krakow. Throughout the various scenes, what struck me was the one concerning the participation in Vatican II of the young vicar capitular (September 16, 1962), afterward auxiliary bishop (January 13, 1964), of Krakow. He gave a valuable contribution to the work of that memorable assembly, and especially drew from it the motivation to engage in the dialogue the Church has maintained with mankind and modern culture. I am therefore very grateful to the reverend president of the Theology Faculty and to the Director of the Institute for the Documentation and Study of the Pontificate of John Paul II, whom I greet warmly, for having given me the chance to participate in these days of study. During these days, thanks to the contributions of illustrious teachers and other ecclesiastical persons, what will become clear are the constant efforts of the great pontiff to implement the teachings of the Council in a coherent way, not only according to the spirit but also according to the letter of the conciliar documents.

One Sweeping Act of Renewal within the Church

Going through the subjects of the various presentations, it is not difficult to get an overview of the extensive act of renewal brought about within the Church by Pope John Paul II, and an indication of which of the directives he used to launch the new evangelization. "Christ—Church—mankind" form an inseparable trilogy within the scope of his teaching. His teaching was enriched by his previous experience as a philosophy professor and as a pastor who was always attentive to the human condition and to humanity's existential anxieties, and enhanced even more decisively by his participation in the Council from the first day to the last. His participation—which he speaks about in his book *Crossing the Threshold of Hope*—was "a unique occasion for listening to others, but also for creative thinking," and again, "a great experience of the Church; it was—as we said at the time—the seminary of the Holy Spirit" (p. 159). From listening to the presentations, with subjects so rich in nuance, there will emerge, I am sure, the character traits of a pastor who tried to put into practice what the Church brings to light in the documents of Vatican II, especially in the two constitutions on the Church: the dogmatic constitution *Lumen Gentium*, and *Gaudium et Spes*, which speaks of the Church in dialogue with the world. The young Bishop Wojtyła collaborated passionately in drafting this latter document, which he goes into in great detail in the aforementioned book, *Crossing the Threshold of Hope*. Therefore, my involvement will confine itself to emphasizing the value and significance of the event we are inaugurating. It is an opportunity to confirm that the entire pontificate of this great pope "breathed" the authentic spirit of the Council, which we must speak about—as noted by the pope in his book—"in order to interpret it correctly and defend it from tendentious interpretations."

Sources of Renewal

The experience of the Council marked the then pastor of the Archdiocese of Krakow in a deep way: the fact that he was allowed to participate in all of the conciliar sessions was a true grace of God. Once he had returned to Poland, he began to implement the directives of the Council enthusiastically. We can understand the spirit that motivated and animated him from the intriguing book that he wrote in 1972 as a handbook on implementing Vatican II: *U podstaw odnowy*. It was translated into Italian and published in 2007 with a preface by Cardinal Camillo Ruini, entitled *Alle fonti del rinnovamento* (and published in English as *Sources of Renewal: The Implementation of Vatican II*). It is a "work study"—as the author himself defined it— or a *vademecum* of the Council. Its aim was to organize the great richness of the conciliar teaching, and it is essential for understanding the "key" Cardinal Wojtyła used to carry out his work and the goal he was trying to achieve. It is a book whose deepest premise—as noted in the introduction by Cardinal Stanislaw Nagy and Prof. Adam Kubis—represents a response to the subsequent questions on faith and on the entire existence of the person of faith:

> What does it mean to be a Christian and to live in the Church and the modern world? These are the existential questions, because they don't just address the truth of the faith, and therefore of pure doctrine, but find their place in the consciousness and tangible existence of every individual, requiring that we decide what attitudes we need to have in order to live as a believing Catholic. (p. xiii)

The book is presented as a sort of synthesis of the various aspects of conciliar doctrine and undoubtedly constitutes a valuable tool for understanding how much the experience of the Council influenced his pastoral work throughout his long pontificate.

How Was the Council Received?

When speaking of the Council, a problem always arises as to how to interpret and apply its decisions. From immediately after the Council, there existed a vibrant renewal movement in the Church, which certainly bore positive fruit. But there were also considerable distortions, which at times became somewhat disturbing. Even today, the decrees of the Council have not become the shared heritage of every Christian community, but have remained documents open only to the few, and sometimes—as I mentioned—they have been interpreted in a misleading way. This has been a concern of the Holy Father, Pope Benedict XVI. In his address to the Roman Curia as part of his Christmas greetings, on December 22, 2005 (forty years after the close of the Council), he tackled this very issue, which is so close to his heart, quite clearly.

He began by asking these questions: "Why has the implementation of the Council, in large parts of the Church, thus far been so difficult? What still remains to be done?" For Benedict XVI, everything depends on the correct interpretation of the Council, or—as we now say—on the correct hermeneutics, on the right key for reading and applying it. The Holy Father's address is both interesting and clear, and it is worth summarizing the main points. It begins with an example that is not necessarily applicable to what has happened in recent years, but could present a certain analogy: it is the description that the great Doctor of the Church, St. Basil, gives regarding the position of the Church directly after the Council of Nicaea, comparing it to a naval battle in the darkness of a storm. St. Basil notes: "Harsh rises the cry of the combatants encountering one another in dispute; already all the Church is almost full of the inarticulate screams, the unintelligible noises, rising from the ceaseless agitations that divert the right rule of the doctrine of true religion, now in the direction of excess, now in that of defect" (*De Spiritu Sancto*, XXX, 77; PG 32, 213 A; SCh 17bis, New Advent, 524).

Two Different Hermeneutics of the Council

In the post-conciliar years, two interpretations, two contrary hermeneutics, have been at odds: one has caused confusion; the other, silently but ever more visibly, has borne fruit. The first, "the hermeneutic of discontinuity and rupture," sometimes holds sway among the mass media and has many adherents in modern theology; the second, "the hermeneutic of reform," proposes renewal through continuity. The hermeneutic of discontinuity—which Benedict XVI warns against—is in danger of causing a rupture between the pre-conciliar Church and the post-conciliar Church. It is worth quoting Benedict XVI's actual words on the subject:

> It asserts that the documents of the Council themselves are not the true expression of the spirit of the Council. They are the result of compromises in which, in order to achieve unanimity, one had to take retrograde steps and reaffirm many old and useless things. However, it is not in these compromises that we see the true spirit of the Council but in the impulses toward the new that undergird the documents: only those represent the true spirit of the Council, and we must go forward beginning with them and in conformity with them. It is because the documents reflect the true spirit of the Council and its newness only in an imperfect way, that we must go forward courageously beyond the documents, making space for innovation in which we can express the Council's deeper intention, even if indistinctly. In a nutshell: we must follow the spirit of the Council, not its documents. (*Insegnamenti* [*Teachings*], vol. 1 [2005], 1024–25)

The True Spirit of the Council

So what is the true spirit of the Council? There is room for interpretation and, consequently, room for applying it creatively. The Council—to again quote the pope—

> can be considered as a type of constitution that abolishes an old constitution and creates a new one. But a constitution needs a mandator who then confirms it, that is the people for whom the constitution is drawn up. The Fathers

did not have such a mandate, and no one ever gave them one; no one, in fact, could give them a mandate because the essential constitution of the Church comes from the Lord and it has been given so that we may reach eternal life. The Bishops, through the sacrament they have received, are trustees of the gift of the Lord and "administrators of the mystery of God" (1 Cor 4:1). (*Insegnamenti* [*Teachings*], vol. 1 [2005], 1024)

In contrast to the hermeneutic of discontinuity is what His Holiness Benedict XVI calls "the hermeneutic of reform," which expresses well the intentions of John XXIII as put forward in his opening address to the Council on October 11, 1962, and then those of Pope Paul VI outlined clearly in his closing address of December 7, 1965. (Today, in fact, marks the fiftieth anniversary of the start of John XXIII's pontificate.) The hermeneutic of reform affirms that the Council intended to "transmit doctrine that was pure and integral, without reduction or misrepresentation." Quoting John XXIII's opening address, the pope continues: "'Our duty is not only to guard this precious treasure, as we have done down the ages, but to dedicate ourselves with energy and without fear to this work, as our age demands (…). It is necessary that this sure and immutable doctrine, which should be faithfully adhered to, be studied and presented in a way that corresponds to the needs of our times'" (*S. Oec. Conc. Vat. II Constitutiones Decreta Declarationes*, 1974, 863–65).

If we wish to express an established truth in a new way, we need to reflect upon it anew and engender a vital relationship with it once more. We need to be aware that the new teaching can mature only if it is born out of an understanding that is conscious of the truth contained in it. We need to also be aware that reflection on the faith demands—as Benedict XVI points out—that we live that faith. In this sense, the program proposed by Pope John XXIII was extremely demanding, just like the synthesis between faithfulness and creative dynamism. But wherever this interpretation has oriented the work of *aggiornamento* in conformance with the Council, what comes to light are the many fruits of holiness and apostolic life.

The Subject of Modern Anthropology

Again Benedict XVI continues: "In the great dispute over mankind, which characterizes modern times, the Council had to address itself in a particular way to the subject of anthropology" (*Insegnamenti* [*Teachings*], vol. 1 [2005], 1026). It had to define the relationship between the Church and the modern age in a new way, a relationship that began in a problematic way with Galileo, and was fractured further when Kant defined "religion within the confines of reason," and when, in the radical phase of the French Revolution, a model of the state and mankind was put forward that left no room for the Church or for faith. In the nineteenth century a difficult conflict took place between radical liberalism, which claimed that natural science embraces the whole of reality, thus rendering superfluous the "hypothesis of God," and the Church, which, under Pius IX, condemned the spirit of the modern age. After that followed years of mutual diffidence and inflexibility, but as the years passed—and we are now in the twentieth century—the outworking of the social doctrine of the Church and the progressive opening of the natural sciences to God marked a process of mutual *rapprochement*. While the natural sciences worked from a method that was limited to the empirical aspect of reality, they became ever more aware that this method could not encompass the whole of reality. So it became clear that there were three types of issues to which the Council had to find solutions: to define in a new way the relationship between faith and modern science; to clarify the relationship between Church and the modern state; and, linked to that subject, to examine the problem of religious tolerance, which itself demanded a new definition of the relationship between the Christian faith and world religions.

Karol Wojtyła's Vision of the Council

The question is, What vision of the Council did Karol Wojtyła have? From each of his contributions as archbishop of Krakow and even more as pontiff, it is easy to see that the conciliar decrees did not mark a break with the past, but are an invitation to pastors to translate the Gospel message in ways that are intelligible to the modern age. This work does not modify the essence of the truths contained in the unchangeable faith, but the method of presenting it to people of every era. One can see that this is the way that the Servant of God John Paul II received the Second Vatican Council. I will briefly outline some of his work.

In 1985, in order to mark the twenty years since the close of the Council, he called an extraordinary Synod of Bishops, and there the bishops were quick to observe the "lights and shades" that had characterized the post-conciliar period. He presented the deliberations of the synod in the letter *Tertio Millennio Adveniente*, in preparation for the Great Jubilee of 2000, affirming that "the examination of conscience cannot fail to include also how we accepted the Council" (n. 36). The concern of Pope John Paul II was always therefore that of safeguarding the genuine intention of the Council Fathers of salvaging, not superseding, those "premature and partial interpretations," which in fact would be an obstacle to expressing the freshness of the teaching of the Council.

A Challenge Taken Up with Courage

Pope John Paul II delivered an address on February 27, 2000, at an international study assembly on how to implement the Council. He affirmed that the Council was first of all "an experience of faith for the Church," and in fact—and I quote—"an act of abandonment to God who emerges, from a clear reading of Acts, as paramount." And he went on to say that anyone who wished to approach the Council without this key to understanding it "robbed himself of any chance of penetrating to its deepest spirit." Furthermore, he continued, the Council was a real challenge for the Council Fathers, which meant—and again I quote—"undertaking a more intimate understanding, in a period of rapid change, of the nature of the Church and its relationship with the world and providing the necessary *aggiornamento*." And he added, referring to his own personal memories: "We have taken up this challenge—I was there with the Council Fathers—and we responded seeking a more coherent understanding of the faith. What we achieved at the Council was to make manifest that modern mankind, if it wants to understand itself more deeply, needs Jesus Christ and the Church, which remains in the world as a sign of unity and of communion" (*Insegnamenti* [*Teachings*], vol. xxiii/1, 273–74). And, furthermore, to see the Council as a break with the past is decidedly misleading.

Time and again during that memorable talk, he reiterated the words of Paul VI who, opening the fourth session, defined the Council thus: "A great and tripartite act of love," an act of love "for God, for the Church, for mankind" (*Insegnamenti* [*Teachings*], vol. iii [1965], 475). John Paul II added that the efficacy of that act has not been exhausted, but continues to operate through the rich dynamic of its teachings.

Christ, Church, Mankind

Let us turn then briefly to the aforementioned extraordinary assembly of the Synod of Bishops. On November 24, 1985, in opening it, John Paul II affirmed: "The Council, which has given us a rich ecclesiological doctrine, has organically drawn together its teaching on the Church with its teaching on the vocation of mankind in Christ" (*Insegnamenti* [*Teachings*], vol. viii 2, 1371). "Christ, Church, Mankind" is once again the subject of this assembly. The pastoral constitution *Gaudium et Spes*—which was very dear to this pontiff— poses fundamental questions to which every person is called to respond, and never ceases to repeat these timeless words: "Only in the mystery of the Incarnate Word does the mystery of man take on light" (n. 22), a message that Pope John Paul II wished to repeat in the fundamental passages of his teaching, because it marked the "true synthesis to which the Church must always look whenever it dialogues with human beings of this as of every other time." As soon as the Council had finished, Bishop Karol Wojtyła wrote:

> Considering the whole of the conciliar teaching, we see that the Church's pastors aimed (...) not only to answer this question: what must we believe in, what is the true sense of this or that truth of the faith, and so on, but attempted rather to answer the more complex question:

what does it mean to be a believer, to be Catholic, to be a member of the Church? (*Sources of Renewal*, 5)

For him, therefore, the Second Vatican Council was the Council "of the Church," "of Christ," "of mankind." These words describe the exact relationship that exists between the ecclesiology, Christology, and anthropology of Vatican II. To speak of Christ is to speak of the Church and therefore of mankind: the one necessarily requires the other because one cannot divide the story of redemption up into categories that have nothing to do with both our personal and community history.

The Blessing of Benedict XVI

In closing, I again give all of you the blessing of His Holiness Benedict XVI, which he already conveyed to you in his message, in which he expresses satisfaction for your having chosen a subject that unites together two issues in which he has a singular interest: on the one hand, Vatican II, in which he had the honor of participating as an expert, and on the other, his beloved predecessor John Paul II, who gave such a significant personal contribution as a conciliar Father and became thereafter, by the will of God, its primary executor during the years of his pontificate. To the wishes expressed by His Holiness Benedict XVI in his message, I unite best wishes for the success of this your international assembly, which will help to keep alive, not only the memory, but also the teaching and the spirit that animated John Paul II. It will also help not only to deepen, but also to renew your dedicated participation in the life of the Church through witnessing with renewed courage to our faith in Christ.

May Mary, wonderful Icon of the Church and Mother of Christ's disciples, to whom John Paul II had dedicated his whole self, be with us during these days of study and make them fruitful. To all of you: God bless your work!

JOHN PAUL II: POPE OF HUMAN RIGHTS

HON. ROCCO BUTTIGLIONE
Senator of the Republic

The subject of mankind and the passion for each person are at the center of the teaching of John Paul II, as also are the reflections of the philosopher Karol Wojtyła, which developed and grew over the course of the years. Here we see two threads of thought: on the one hand, the great reflection on the Council; on the other, a completely Polish element, whose roots come from Paweł Włodkowic and which received significant development in the Lublin school. We remember here the names Mieczesław Krapiec, Jerzy Kalinowski, Stanisław Kaminski, and many others who have dedicated their teaching and research activities to the subject of the human person, its dignity and its rights.

The Subject of Freedom and Truth

We begin today's reflection with two works by Karol Wojtyła: *Osoba i czyn* (*Person and Act*), the fundamental work that condenses the philosophical thoughts of Karol Wojtyła, and *U podstaw odnowy* (*Sources of Renewal*), the work that offers his reading of the Council.

They say that Albino Luciani, then Pope John Paul I of blessed memory, had his curiosity piqued during the work of the Council by a young Polish bishop who, during the debates, as he was listening to the presentations, was at the same time writing with great concentration. He asked who the young bishop was and what he was writing: it was Karol Wojtyła and he was writing *Osoba i czyn*.

13

We do not know if this story is true. If it's not true, it may as well be. It underlines the fact that that book came into existence from the sessions of the Council and is, in its roots, a reflection on the Council. Although it is a work of pure philosophy, whose structure is very technical and which makes rigorous use of the tools of philosophical reason—nevertheless, the concern that enlivens it is to offer that philosophical renewal that the Council needed in order to completely develop its potential, and to reach modern human beings in a convincing way with the news of salvation. Hence, the need for complementarity with *U podstaw odnowy*, a work explicitly dedicated to the appropriation of the conciliar teachings.

Dignitatis Humanae is central to the Council. It constitutes the full recognition, by the Catholic Church, of the principle of religious freedom and, more generally, *the way of freedom*.

In the eighteenth and nineteenth centuries, Catholics were attacked (sometimes with good reason) as enemies of freedom, particularly enemies of religious freedom. The conflict between Catholicism and modernity stems, in large part, from the topic of freedom. The Church defends the rights of objective truth, and this defense necessarily and irreducibly seems to place her in opposition to the rights of freedom of thought. Therefore, this is the question: Is it possible to reconcile the rights of freedom with the rights of truth? Is it possible to do so in a way that does not lead to renouncing the Christian proclamation's claims to truth? That is, is it possible to achieve an affirmation of the rights of freedom in a way that does not lead to yielding to relativism but to deepening the truth of the Christian experience? An adequate response to this question requires deep reflection not only on the meaning of truth and freedom but also, even more profoundly, on what (or who) man is.

Underlying all this is the great question of idealism and subjectivism. If objective truth does not exist, then truth is simply whatever the individual recognizes as such. The individual creates truth. The individual is, essentially, the great and fascinating discovery of modernity. Catholics are, in large part, opposed to that discovery. The Council is the occasion for a great rethinking. As we have said, that rethinking focuses on mankind.

In reality, the question is even more radical. It concerns God. Man is, in fact, the visible image of the invisible God. Thus, the way

we understand humanity and the way we understand God are necessarily the same. This is a radical rethinking. It is crucial that this
reassessment arises not from giving in to the spirit of the age, to the
mentality of this world, but from an in-depth study of the Christian
message.

The Human Person and Its Dignity

Let us begin from the vision and experience of God. We make
reference to the first work of Wojtyła, his degree thesis on *Quaestio
de fide apud S. Johannem a Sancta Cruce* and which (together with his
first encyclical as pope, *Redemptoris Hominis*) contains in equal parts
the spirit and the plan for his whole pontificate. The first encyclical
of Pope Benedict XVI, *Deus Caritas Est*, also makes reference to this.

Philosophy can say little about God. It can say that there is a
God, it can discern his presence in the order of creation, but it cannot
see his face. In this way, philosophy is open to the possibility of revelation, as Plato has already said in *Phaedo*: how good it would be if
Someone, from the other side of the sea of this life, were to come to
clarify our doubts and respond to our hopes. The God of Jesus Christ
is that response. Who the Father is, no one can know. The Son, who
alone knows the face of the Father, has revealed it. This revelation is
not in opposition to human reason, even if it goes beyond its limits
and is not identified with it.

The God of Jesus Christ is a Trinitarian God; he is a God in
three Persons. In order to understand how he can be both one and
three, the theologians of the fourth and fifth centuries had to rethink
the subject of relation, and, consequently, of person. I am what I am,
but I am also what I have become throughout the course of my life
in relation to those who have loved me and whom I love. So also with
those whom I have not been able to, or wanted to, love—those whom
I have hated or who hated me. Even my body is the result of a relationship between a man and a woman, between my father and
mother. The person is a being who lives holding within himself the
presence of another.

God also is person. More accurately, God is "person" in a
strong and native sense and we are "person" in a weak and derivative

sense, through participation or indeed by image and resemblance. Each one of the persons in the Trinity lives in relation to the other two in a way so radical that it has no substance or consistency without that relationship.

Man too, as we have said, is person. One lives within the other. The personality of the human person is fundamentally communal. We were made to love and to be loved, to become members, one of the other. However, there is a radical division in man. There is a weight that compels the human person to affirm self in opposition to another person, and even so far as a contempt for God. The communion that is fulfilled in the eternal bond within the Trinity is not found in human history.

This is why God became man in the person of Jesus Christ. As man (the new Adam), he has begun a new history. That man, Jesus of Nazareth, is capable of a radical friendship with every person and the whole human being. He is capable of a perfect acceptance that changes the lives of those who allow him to accept them. By entering into friendship with him, they enter into communion with each other. How can those who let their whole lives be redefined by the presence of Christ not be one?

At the same time, by entering into communion with each other through Jesus of Nazareth, they enter into communion with God's own life. The history of man becomes then the history of salvation in which they become a new people, the Church, as the birth of a new humanity reconciled with itself and with God.

All this was achieved through the cross of Christ.

Let us stop for a moment to reflect on the mystery of the cross. Jesus could have asked the Father for freedom from suffering and death, and the Father would have sent twelve legions of angels. Twelve legions of angels are how many it would take, not only to free Jesus from the cross and reconquer the kingdom of Israel, but to conquer the whole world.

Jesus, however, does not ask for twelve legions of angels to intervene. He does not want to conquer the world by imposing his power on the people. He wants to conquer the heart of every person by their passing through his freedom. Time and again the question that resounds through history is, "How is it possible for God to exist and be all-good while the world is dominated by hatred and pain?"

Hatred and pain exist because humanity is wicked, and God does not wish to impose truth and justice from outside by force. The God of Jesus Christ wants to conquer the heart of every person by their passing through the narrow gate of his freedom.

God exists, objective truth exists, as does the law of God—holy and venerable, revealed on Sinai but also written on the heart of every person. Nevertheless, the law cannot save, and even truth cannot save if it does not come from the heart or if the works of the law arise from fear and not from a renewed heart. This is the drama of man's freedom and of salvation. This is the drama of grace.

Freedom of Conscience

We will see now how the need to respect the freedom of mankind cannot be embraced by Christian faith from the outside but comes out of its very roots. Our God is like a young man who is courting a young woman and knows that he cannot constrain love, nor can he force it or buy it. Anyone who tries to do so destroys love from its very roots. He seeks love by proving his love and even by placing his own life in the balance, *usque ad mortem, mortem autem cruces*. Therefore, the responsibility of the Church is not simply to proclaim the truth, but to witness to it in a convincing way, holding out freedom for every single human person.

Behind this understanding of God and of mankind, St. Thomas Aquinas formulates one of the fundamental principles of moral philosophy (and of theology): *bonum ex integra causa, malum ex quocumque defecto*. In order to carry out a moral act, two elements are required: one has to do the right thing and one has to do it for the right reason. The objective element is conformity with the truth of things, with the law, which expresses the will of God. The subjective element is the reason for which the right thing is done: love of God. It is not a good deed if we do the right thing but for the wrong reason, out of fear and out of love. Equally, it is not a good deed if we do the wrong thing for the right reason.

Objectivism within moral theology risks equating the Christian moral with the moral of the Pharisee, transforming it into a moral of the law. Subjectivism within moral theology (criticized quite rightly by Professor Father Andrzej Szostek in his book *Natura rozum wolność*) runs the risk of forgetting that Jesus did not come to abolish the law but to renew it from within, requiring that his precepts be fulfilled in love that presupposes freedom.

It is true that a certain privilege is given to the objective fact of an action. St. Thomas Aquinas says the same, that *coscientia erronea obligat*. A person must always act in accordance with his or her conscience, even if it happens to be wrong. This expression, to which some have tried to attribute profound significance, giving it a subjective twist, in reality expresses a rather banal truth. A person does wrong without knowing it is wrong. If he knew, he would not do wrong. If he insists on doing wrong knowing that it is wrong, his conscience would not be mistaken but wicked. It is not possible to arrive at a relativist outcome from this aphorism of St. Thomas. A person who does wrong in good faith wants to correct his error, and his best friend is not the person who colludes with his error but the person who helps him to correct it. Everyone has the duty to seek the truth with all their heart, that is, they have a duty to form their conscience. If they do not find the truth because they are not looking for it, then the erroneous conscience is also to blame.

Wojtyła sees the Council as an event that is primarily *pedagogical*, or rather, more precisely, *pastoral*. The Council is not dogmatic; no new dogma was proclaimed and furthermore, none of the Church's dogmas were renounced. This changes the way in which the kerygma is announced. The method is not deductive but rather *inductive*. It begins with the experience of the person and here the phenomenological method is of some help. A method that is more adapted to the nature of the content has to be developed, and if that content is Christian freedom, the method must be one of freedom. This theological vision, which is the vision of the Council, is reflected both in the book *U podstaw odnowy* and in the teaching of John Paul II, beginning with the programmatic encyclical of his pontificate, *Redemptor Hominis*.

This theological vision engenders, although without delineating details, a study of the same anthropological reflection, returning to the question: What (Who) is man? Karol Wojtyła tries to answer this question in his other great book, *Osoba i czyn*.

The human person is primarily a being who is called to the truth and called to recognize it as truth. We recall a book by the great Austrian theologian Karl Rahner: *Hörer des Wortes* (*Hearers of the Word*). The thing that makes us specifically human is being capable of truth. St. Thomas Aquinas tells us that the person is an *ens intelligens et liberum*. Intelligence, which characterizes the person, is precisely that: the capacity for truth. But what is freedom? Freedom is the ability to give, or withhold, one's assent to known truth. Correspondingly, Wojtyła identifies in the human being the conscience's (*świadomość*) capacity for self-consciousness (*samowiedza*). The conscience has the ability to reflect, internalize, and live the known truth, internally taking it as its own. In this way the known truth becomes properly *recognized*.

Here Wojtyła places under critical examination the discovery of subjectivism and conscience that stands at the center of modernity. Through the act of the conscience's recognizing, the person loves and then revises and restates the known truth within its own interior world. The person creates that interior world, gives form to its inner self, and becomes then either good or evil *from the moral point of view*, that is, simply and altogether *good as a man*.

The modern claim of creativity, subjectivism, and the human conscience is accepted by Wojtyła but also profoundly reworked. The human person is creative because the world in which we live is not simply the world God created. It is the world recreated by mankind through its work. The work of mankind does not, however, take place in a vacuum. It is always applied to a substance that preceded it, and this substance has its own nature, which humanity must discover in order to allow its potential to bear fruit. If human beings do not know the objective structure of the materials to which they apply their work, that work remains ineffective or achieves results different, or even opposite, from what was intended. Work poses a cognitive problem not just in terms of pragmatic effectiveness but also in terms of the adoption of moral responsibility. It is, in fact, possible to know reality in a correct way and then make morally wrong use of something by going against what has been learned. Mankind has a duty to the order of values, which themselves are also capable of being known.

CHRIST, CHURCH, MANKIND

The Subject of Human Rights

We can and must exploit nature to satisfy our needs and wants but in doing so we also have a duty to preserve, respect, and enhance its beauty and to preserve its fecundity for future generations.

Human action—Wojtyła teaches us—is creative not only insofar as it changes (for better or worse) the world around us, for it also changes us, the individuals who carry out the action, making us human beings who are either better or worse. In fact, through our conscience, we internalize the world in which we live and create our own individual world, while at the same time contributing to building the human intersubjective world, the common world of life. Even in this case, the individual is a creator but not in the absolute sense. The human being is, in fact, a creator based on an objective truth that can and should be recognized. The subject of creativity and of establishing the world of life beginning from each person's lived experience, which is typical of modern thought and particularly of phenomenology, can be accepted, but not in opposition to the concept of being and objective truth. This is better considered as emerging from the fundamental concept of truth and the individual's ability to know the truth.

The establishment of external reality through work and also mankind's ability to internalize through acts of conscience do not come about—indeed, cannot come about—arbitrarily but must be based on what is. That which is, on the other hand, is not a reality that is given once for all and that remains unaffected by mankind's actions and human creativity. That which is requires, at its very core, to be known, properly understood or completed, and integrated in its true sense, through intelligent and free action. The world outside of us has a structure that human actions must respect. And we ourselves have our own internal structure, whether physical or psychological, that we too can know and have a duty to respect. Therefore, mankind is not, as in idealist philosophy, *pure creativity*. What we can say, if anything, is that the human being is a freedom incarnate, which always carries with it its own position in the order of nature and for which position it always remains responsible.

It is on the basis of this rich philosophical, anthropological, and theological process that John Paul II confronts the issue of human

20

rights, and this differentiates his vision of human rights from that of others, which have received and continue to receive an ample hearing in our society.

There exists, in the usual way in which we speak of human rights, a strange paradox. The human person whose rights are asserted is a being without nature and the rights that that person claims (*rectius*: which are claimed for that person) cannot be rooted in human nature. The fundamental problem of today's discussion on human rights is that in some ways their roots are based on a void. Because of this, their characteristics are unstable, easily manipulated by anyone, and, in the end, most effectively manipulated by defenders of social power. Depending on what way we view the world, we attribute to human beings some rights but not others, or perhaps we determine that they are human beings and therefore deserve rights; but only some human beings and not others.

The first question is central to the discussion on human rights today. Unborn children, embryos: are they or are they not human beings and therefore subject to rights? Objective knowledge, biological science, tells us that they are individuals of the human species. If we consider our conscience to be bound to internalize whatever is offered to it by objective knowledge, it is difficult to deny that they are persons and therefore subject to rights. Our margin of choice is even larger if we maintain that the conscience is free to decide its own contents. In a famous court case in France, a woman was accused of infanticide and important proponents of existentialist culture at the time defended her arguing that she did not, according to her conscience, consider the baby to be a human being.

In a more or less similar way, terrorists argue that their conscience considers political adversaries not as human beings but only as enemies of class or of humanity. If we start down that slippery slope, then it is just as possible, on the other hand, for some people to consider animals to be persons, or at least some animals. The spread of so-called animalism, which can be found even in the philosophy of Peter Singer, shows that this assertion finds confirmation in the reality of our times. In every case, the limits of the human are established in a way that is necessarily arbitrary, with the possible result that humanity becomes a movable feast, which plays out in different ways with different individuals.

The same problem of the exact definition of who is a person and who deserves rights arises at the end of life. Some refuse to *consider as a person* an individual of the human species who does not satisfy certain conditions, for example, if they are in a coma. That, they say, is not life. Instead of reflecting on the objective facts offered by medical science (the person is alive *and* is in a coma, even if it is irreversible), they attempt to violate the facts with an arbitrary construct. It is no surprise that they say, *For me*, this is not life. Which means, I don't feel like going to the bother of confronting myself with this life and facing the questions that it poses to my conscience.

A second question that can be asked in this regard has not so much to do with defining who is human and therefore deserving of human rights, but rather with defining what goes to make up those rights. To what does a human being have rights? If we maintain that a human being is defined as having a conscience, it is obvious that they cannot have predefined rights. A human being is what he or she decides to be and therefore has whatever rights he or she decides to have. The fundamental right, or indeed the only right that remains and contains within itself all the others, is the right to nondiscrimination.

Obviously nondiscrimination is important and none of us wants to be discriminated against; nevertheless, it is very dangerous to consider the right to nondiscrimination as absolute. The right to nondiscrimination derives from the principle of equality. From the time that we are children we protest when, for example, our parents give a gift to our brothers or sisters and do not give us anything. By protesting like this, we are demonstrating the conviction that we have a dignity equal to that of our brothers or sisters and have the right to be treated in the same way.

And yet, sometimes our parents do not listen to us and insist on treating their children in different ways, even if we protest. Let us imagine (and this often happens in reality) that a boy protests because his brother receives a birthday gift and he wants one too, and he is sad because he feels discriminated against. Is his protest legitimate? Obviously not, because it was his brother's birthday and not his. In this case, there is a difference between the two brothers that makes them (from this point of view) unequal. It is possible to be equal but still be considerably different. One of the most important differences is merit. Let us imagine that one of the boys has done something for the common good, for example, he has washed the dishes or cut the grass on the lawn in front of the house. His brother cannot legitimately ask to be rewarded in the same way. Not if the reward is earned.

Aristotle correctly explains that it is right to treat equal situations in an equal way and different situations in a different way. This is the correct formulation of the principle of equality. Each one of us has a gender-specific body, and is therefore either male or female. A decisive element of our development, of our cultural growth, is how this reality, which we know through self-knowledge, is internalized by us and made our own in our conscience. Sexual identity is an objective fact but also a subjective or cultural fact. It is an objective fact that is internalized within our conscience and endorsed by it. There are many ways to live out masculinity or femininity. There are, however, limits. If I am a man, I cannot act as if I were a woman within my conscience, or vice versa. Similarly, I cannot ask that others treat me as such or that the state allow me the right to create a family with someone else of my own sex. In fact, the family has a social function, to have children and educate them. It is a determining social function for the survival and well-being of society. This function presupposes sexual differentiation: a real, not imaginary, sexual difference, not constituted unilaterally and arbitrarily according to one's conscience. Here there is a very good reason to treat different situations in different ways, without it being unjust discrimination.

It seems right, then, to recognize the nature of things, against which the measure of right and wrong can be judged and from which emerges the sphere of natural rights. Natural rights are rights that emerge from the nature of something and human rights are rights that correspond to the nature of a human being.

If we link the idea of rights with the idea of nature, a certain correlation emerges between rights and duties. The first and fundamental right of every human being is to do his duty, to carry out those actions to which his nature destines him. In the case of the human being, what are those actions?

The proper action of a human being, what makes one human, is to seek the truth, to know it, and to live according to the known truth. Seeking the truth is not just an intellectual pursuit. When human beings seek for truth, there is necessarily a moment of risk and experimentation. Whatever I know will be put to the test in life, and the experiences of life will either confirm me in that truth or cause me to place it in doubt. Experience guides the quest for truth. There is therefore a circular movement that goes from seeking, to knowing, to life experience, and then leads back again to seeking. There is no end to seeking the truth. Therefore, the first and fundamental right of the human being is freedom, which begins with freedom of conscience. This contains within itself the right to err. We are not speaking here about the right to err as being on the same level as the truth. We are speaking about the right that every human being has to commit errors because in the dynamic process of the human search for truth even error is (or can be) a stage on the path toward the truth.

The Relationship Between Public and Private

Although the actions of a human being are concerned with his or her social nature and the tension between the individual and the community, there are nevertheless some acts that are polarized to one side of that tension or the other. Actions that are exclusively concerned with, or seem to be concerned with, the individual person fall within the area of their responsibility. We can say that those actions are carried out entirely within the personal area and pertain to it. Actions that are to be found at the community end of the spectrum and that influence the lives of others require freedom to be exercised in relation to the freedom of other members of the community. Here the free will of the individual must be constrained and even impinged upon; it must learn to exercise its freedom *together with others and respecting the freedom of others.*

While this private sphere is subject to moral judgment, the public sphere is subject not only to moral judgment but also to juridical control. Can we say, therefore, that the private lies within the scope of freedom, while the public comes under the authority of the state? No, in the public sphere, the right to freedom does not disappear, in fact, but is expressed in the right to *participation*— to not simply be subject to decisions taken by an external authority of whatever kind, but to participate, in ways and forms that are appropriate, in the decisions being made with regard to us. What we are concerned with is the foundation of the principles of political order and in a particular way of democratic political order.

What we require of political order is not only that it make just decisions, oriented toward the common good of the community; we also require (and this is new with regard to a certain previous doctrine) that the decisions be made in a way in which all citizens can participate. In that way, citizens are called to internalize within their conscience the decisions taken, to take ownership of them, and to see them as an expression of their own freedom.

This principle of participation is valid not only in the area of the state but also in the areas of work, the family, and any human community. Wherever human beings cannot participate, they can never feel that a decision is taken with their participation, and they are alienated, deprived of the opportunity to experience their dignity in the decision and their communion with other human beings.

This, as we have seen, is a change to a previous doctrine that highlighted the role of the common good in the community and in political decision-making, and did not consider equally the significance of participation or, if you like, the role of the conscience and of subjectivism in political action. Both the actions of the individual and the role of the human community have a twofold outcome: they change, for good or ill, the external environment in the individual or community they affect, but they also change the individual himself and the community itself that are subject to the action. An action taken without participation cannot be truly human, even if it is right from an objective point of view. It weakens the interior bond the individual has with the community, and the individual does not experience his or her own humanity. A just political order is oriented toward the common good but is also oriented toward the common good in *the right way*, that is, regarding the human right to participation.

We have up to now defined the right to freedom and the right to participation, that is, the social dimension of the right to freedom. Correspondingly, we have differentiated the private sphere from the public. We have also shown how freedom is different from willfulness. Freedom seeks truth; willfulness turns in on itself and renounces the search for truth. Freedom wants to find truth in order to make the truth; willfulness wishes that truth did not exist so that it could *do whatever it pleased* rather than *what is right*. We have, in this way, introduced the concept that it is from the nature of things that mankind derives its rights. There exists the right to do that which corresponds to the nature of things. What does not exist is the right to do things that contradict the nature of things. In saying this, naturally there are limits: human beings have the right to err. There is no right to stop someone from erring, but neither is there a right to aid and abet someone in erring. In the private sphere, each person has, as I have said, the right to err. In the public sphere, however, we have a duty to form legislation that corresponds to the nature of things. To return to the example of homosexuality, it is one thing to say that it is not a crime and that a man has the freedom to practice it. However, it is another to ask that the state promote it as a lifestyle equivalent to marriage and the family. Here the nature of the family must be respected and, because of that, the family has the right to be encouraged and promoted by public authority in a different way from other forms of sexual expression and cohabitation that must remain within the scope of private autonomy.

In order to understand and to study these subjects better, we must move forward on this theme of rights.

Family, Nation, State

The individual is a being that is composed of a body and a spirit in an indissoluble way. In order to be free and to seek for truth, the individual must *be* and must *live*. It does not make sense to talk about the right to freedom and the right to truth if we are not at the same time talking about the right to life. The right to life is more than the right not to be killed. It is also the right not to die of hunger, which itself is more than the right not to be considered useless by others, but rather the right to earn a living. A just law is a law in which each person can earn a living through work.

Sex is the greatest force that God has invented (in the order of nature) for placing human beings together and allowing them to experience that they are ordained to be members of a community and can completely fulfill themselves only through a free gift of self. To live the experience of love, of marriage, of fatherhood and motherhood is also a fundamental human right, over and above that of being of fundamental importance to society. This right marks the transition point between mere individual rights and the rights of the community in which the individual grows as a person. Here we are dealing with the right to form a family, which is a community that has rights that correspond to the growth and the mutual encounter of the rights of the members of which it is composed. The family is a natural community founded on marriage, that is, on the love and commitment of a man and a woman to live together, to sustain each other through the trials of life, and to bear children and educate them. Today the family is under attack from political and social systems. The state is concerned for the individuals who make up a family, but not for the family itself.

It is impossible to encounter the person and maintain that person in his or her objective rights, all the while ignoring the tangible environment in which the person lives and the network of solidarity into which he or she is integrated. The family has its own rights, has its own *common good*, which must be considered when defining the common good of the greater community. In this regard, the family must represent itself to the state in all social policies. In order to have an effective respect for the rights of the family, a precondition is to define exactly what the family is and is not. We will not go into details on this subject, but we will say that the family is a *natural* community. It is natural because we do not belong to it by choice, but simply by being born. We do not make this community, but in a certain sense it makes us. In our freedom we are called to internalize and relive this original sense of belonging internally.

The family is not the only natural community. In Lublin, in his memorable address, John Paul II reasserted *the rights of the nation*. Just as we are born into a family, so we are also born into a nation, and from it we learn a language and a culture that contain within themselves a specific access route to the truth of humanity. An individual has a right to his or her nation and national culture. Just as an individual has a right to a nation and has a right to participate in the life of that nation, so also the nation has rights of its own. *The nation has the right to sovereignty through the culture.*

Let us pause for a moment on this theme: every nation has the right to develop its culture and to allow its members to participate in it. It is through its culture that the nation properly exercises its sovereignty and carries out its mission in the world. It is obvious how important this principle is in a world in which so many nations suffer the denial of important rights and even the fundamental right to exist.

In saying that the nation exercises sovereignty through its culture, John Paul II at the same time is distinguishing between sovereignty through culture and political sovereignty, and similarly between nation and state. Sometimes history mixes nations together in such a way that it is impossible to establish each of them with its own separate state. They inhabit the same territory and must set up communal state structures.

At other times history creates a particularly close relationship, a kinship in a certain sense, between different nations. For example, particular cultural closeness (common Christian roots), participation in a common economic area (the European Economic Community), and convergent interests in the area of defense and foreign politics have driven European countries to build a common political structure: the European Union. In this structure, each nation has a right to have its own cultural sovereignty respected and, furthermore, each member state has the right to ask the Union to concern itself only with those things that cannot be accomplished effectively at the level of the individual member state (the principle of subsidiarity).

Ultimately, all men form part of a unique human community. Nations and states have a duty to collaborate within the scope of this unique human community. Different cultures and civilizations are not closed in on themselves, but are paths toward the one and only truth about man. In the same way, God has given the Earth to human beings, *all* human beings, so that they can draw sustenance from it, everything necessary to live a life worthy of man. The word *earth* here means not just the Earth in its usual and original sense, but also all instruments of work and wealth production that have accumulated throughout the course of humanity's history. It is natural that the Earth be divided among us in such a way that different states have management and control over different parts of it, just as each individual's right to private property is also natural over individual parts of humanity's productive assets. This diverse division of goods comes about through historical events and also through the industrialization of human beings and their work. Nevertheless, there remains over the whole Earth a *social mortgage*. The whole Earth must be put into service for the lives of all human beings. It is not right that some individuals (or worse, entire peoples) be excluded from this relationship with the Earth's resources. Humanity's principal resource is humanity itself—its intelligence and its capacity for work. It is not right that some individuals (even the majority of humanity) be excluded from the opportunity of adequately developing their own intellectual and moral potential. It is morally unacceptable for entire nations to be practically excluded from participation in scientific research and university schooling.

It is not only natural communities that exist. There are also communities that individuals belong to by free choice, and these communities also have their own rights that should be respected. Particular stature is accorded to communities where individuals come together to live out their relationship with the Absolute. Here we are speaking of religious communities. Respect of their rights is bound strictly to respect for the primary and fundamental right to freedom of conscience. Strictly speaking, the Church in itself is not just a voluntary Christian community. Rather, it is a supernatural community in which the individual internalizes, and confirms through an act of freedom, God's call to communion with him. This call comes even before our conception and birth. As with the example of Jesus, the Church does not require public recognition of its supernatural nature.

Externally, the Church upholds the communal rights of every religious community, without exception. The universal right to freedom of conscience and freedom of religion does not, however, imply that all religious confessions should be treated in exactly the same way. History has created particular links between one religion, one culture, and one land. These links give rise to particular rights that must be equally recognized without, however, damaging the fundamental right to freedom of conscience and religion.

Another voluntary community that merits particular attention is the *community of workers*. The encyclical *Laborem Exercens* is dedicated in a particular way to defending the rights of this community.

In reality, it is not at all clear whether the community of workers is natural or voluntary. In fact, everyone is called to be part of this community, in the form and manner of his own choosing. Besides the family, work is the other great experience in which we learn that we need one another and in which we learn to be members of a community. While we procure the goods necessary for our life and the life of our family, at the same time we help, we must help, our co-workers to achieve the same objective, and we learn a particular form of friendship and participation in each other's lives. In this regard, the community of workers (when it is just and not alienating) is where we *experience great solidarity*.

We see this solidarity reflected also in the *struggle for social justice*, in the war against exploitation of work, against the humiliation of human beings in the process of work, against the marginalization of some workers, and against the loss of the right to live.

Conclusion

We have attempted to convey an idea, even if briefly, of the breadth and also the innovative character of the teaching of John Paul II on natural rights. Its roots are to be found in the teaching of the Council and in the reflections of Wojtyła on the Council and on humanity in the light of the Council.

We have seen how John Paul II places at center stage the dialogue between the freedom of the individual and the freedom of God, the individual's duty to seek and recognize the truth and his right and duty to do so freely. It is not enough to know the truth: we must recognize it and make it the expression of our free subjectivity. From this emerges the dialectic of nature and conscience that governs the entire scope of human rights.

This is the vision of human rights with which John Paul II used to confront three adversaries. The first adversary was communism. Communism does not recognize human rights or natural rights. In his sixth *Thesis on Feuerbach*, Marx explains that the individual is nothing but *a collection of social relationships*. The person is completely absorbed into the mass of humanity and in the march of history. John Paul II opposes this vision with the fact that the worker is a person and wants to live and experience his or her own dignity through work and through social existence. This was the overwhelming force that animated the *Solidarność* movement and the entire rebirth of the Polish nation. In the face of this intellectual and moral resistance, communism collapsed and with it the European and world order (or disorder) that was created by the Yalta agreement.

The second adversary was the Latin American national security dictatorships. These hoped to achieve the common good of the nation, while ignoring subjectivity and the right to participation. These regimes also fell before nonviolent opposition staged in the name of the rights of man and guided by the Catholic Church and by John Paul II.

The third adversary was the moral relativism of the West, which sought to free man from his constituent relationship with the truth. A conscience without truth drives us toward "the last days of humanity," when every community dissolves, babies are not born, and a civilization hastens toward its decline and disappearance. John Paul II countered this culture of decline and death with the World Youth Day to show those who experience youth, and who are called to life, the way to life.

In a special way, the pope's message is directed *toward the youth*. If the fundamental question is the conscience's capacity to perceive the truth and reality, then the first reality in the order of nature is the child. To communicate the greatness of being mothers, to uphold the mission to become mothers, is the fundamental question of our culture. We ask young women to follow a career but no one explains the greatness of motherhood.

Pregnancy often arrives unlooked-for, to challenge our plans, to challenge the way we usually build our individual and social reality. The baby, when it arrives, is the reality that imposes itself on our schemes and forces us to either accept or reject it. Every time a young woman accepts this reality, as the Virgin of Nazareth once did, in some way the hope of the world is renewed.

THE RECEPTION OF VATICAN II IN THE WORK AND DOCUMENTS OF THE SYNOD OF KRAKOW
(1972–1979)

MGR. TADEUSZ PIERONEK

A little less than four months prior to Pope John XXIII's convening Vatican II, Father Karol was created auxiliary bishop of Krakow. He was the youngest bishop in Poland, thirty-eight years of age. He was also a scholar now fully formed, engaged in pastoral work. When he was elevated to the dignity of Peter's successor he said: "The designs of Providence are inscrutable." There is no doubt that this statement could apply equally to Wojtyła's entire life. He came to light at the exact time that the Church and the world had most need of him.

Bishop Wojtyła at the Council

Karol Wojtyła integrated himself into the work of the Council from the moment Pope John XXIII turned to all the bishops for suggestions regarding the subjects with which the Council should concern itself. However, his was not just a simple response to this specific request, so much as a demonstration of his full commitment to the good of the Church. The text he sent to the Council's preparatory committee confirms this. In it he denounced the present humanist crisis, saying that it required deeper reflection and a decisive response on the part of the Council.[1] The fact that an auxiliary bishop took this position on such a fundamental question surely demonstrates that, having adequate knowledge of the issue, he also had the courage to share it with all the bishops of the world in order to draw their attention to the profound transformation that was taking place among the faithful and to the need for the Church to meet the challenges arising from it. That voice was important because it came out of the experience of a world that was held hostage by the doctrines and praxis of a totalitarian system. The Western world did not have any similar experience. The task of the Council was to see clearly in the real conditions in which the life of faith was lived within the various political, economic, and, most importantly, ideological systems.

After the sudden death (in June 1962) of Archbishop Eugeniusz Baziak, archbishop of Lviv—which, by the will of the Apostolic See, governed the Church of Krakow throughout the most difficult years of communist reprisals—Bishop Wojtyła, from his position in Krakow, was named vicar capitular of the Archdiocese of Krakow (on July 16, 1962), and initially participated in the work of the Council in that capacity. The work of the Polish bishops was coordinated by Cardinal Stefan Wyszyński, who indicated the issues that they had to present. Bishop Wojtyła was in this regard autonomous, since he himself chose and wrote his own presentations alone, having evidently many questions that were well thought-out, and were tried and tested from a pastoral point of view. His vision was of a Church open to the world and to humanity, and he was free of the complexes and habits of the past that kept the Church tied to fossilized formulas. He had the student priests of Krakow, who were at his disposal, type out the text of his submission.

Bishop Wojtyła showed a lively interest throughout the conciliar debate, and participated in all the general sessions where he often had the floor and presented written submissions. Here it is not possible to examine his submissions in detail; however, it is worth highlighting that each of them was distinguished by care for the individual person, who is not capable of either understanding himself or completely fulfilling his humanity without Christ. The commitment of Karol Wojtyła to the work of the Council began with his text on the humanist crisis given on December 30, 1959, and presented to the preparatory council. His participation, by this time as archbishop of the City of Krakow, was chiefly in sessions III and IV of the Council.

From the intense work on Scheme XIII emerged the Pastoral Constitution on the Church in the Modern World, *Gaudium et Spes*.

The submissions of Bishop Wojtyła during session I were concerned with the sources of revelation, the major responsibility of baptismal godfathers and godmothers in the religious education of the child, the position of the laity, and the significance of Mary for the life of the Church. Through all these issues, he asked for a new way of looking at the world that took into account the current sensitivity of the faithful and the dignity of the human person, as well as the exceptional role of Mary as Mother of the Son of God. During session II, he pointed out the need for a personal vision of the Church as the community of the people of God and the necessity of including the laity in the outworking of its mission, as well as holiness as the measure of Christian life that is accessible to all. In a particular way he defended the right of every person to religious freedom, rejecting any coercion in this matter as being contrary to human dignity. However, his largest scope was reserved for work on the pastoral constitution *Gaudium et Spes*, which gave him the greatest amount of satisfaction. It was the crowning of his many years of intellectual effort as philosopher, theologian, and pastor, constituting at the same time the response to the requirements and suggestions contained in his contribution on the humanist crisis, and also, most of all, the Church's response to the pressing problems of the contemporary world.

I do not intend here to go into detail about, much less judge, the contributions of Bishop Wojtyła to the Council. That has already been done to a large extent by highly competent writers. However, I still feel that it is important to briefly underline how much he felt responsible for this great event, which the Council undoubtedly was. He translated that responsibility into concern that the community of the Church of Krakow quickly and thoroughly assimilate the results of the Council.

How Vatican II was Received

Bishop Wojtyła began work aimed at the best possible reception of the Second Vatican Council in the diocese even during the Council sessions: through homilies and even through pastoral letters sent from Rome, the faithful were kept fully informed of progress and of the issues being discussed. This proved crucial because in those days the public was not receiving accurate news on religious life. He received no help in this from either the Catholic press, which was subject to censorship and printed only a small number of copies, or from the public means of communication, which misrepresented conciliar thought by presenting this great event as a battlefield in which the traditionalists and those who advocated progress fought for predominance. Bishop Wojtyła experienced the Council as a very significant religious event, in which the Holy Spirit dialogued with the contemporary Universal Church: "The history of the Council, which will be written in full one day, was present in 1962–5 as an extraordinary event in the minds of all the bishops concerned: it absorbed all their thoughts and stimulated their sense of responsibility, as an exceptional and deeply felt experience."[2]

As one of the Council Fathers he felt himself lacking before the Holy Spirit, and the voice of the bishops united through the Council was viewed by him as an authentic expression of what "the Spirit 'said to the Church' at a particular historical moment."[3] He maintained that this lack could be made up only with a response of faith that is a response to the Word of God, and to what the Spirit, through the Council, was saying to the Church.

Following this train of thought, two of his declarations especially seem to assume a particular significance. The first is a small part of his address on March 8, 1964, on entering the cathedral of Wawel after being named archbishop of Krakow. He said:

> From the perspective of my pastoral service I see that we must implement together (…) if you want to refer to it as a program, so be it, we will call it such. There is nothing new in this program; it is simple and very ancient. External things, the things of God, are the simplest and the most profound. There is no need to create new programs; we need only to find new ways, with renewed zeal and renewed availability, of entering into this program and reactivating it according to the needs of our times. The Council is still being developed, but it lives most of all in

this way of thinking. And what I desire is to revive the Archdiocese of Krakow until the spirit of the Council and of the Church lives.[4]

The second declaration can be read in the preface to Cardinal Wojtyła's book entitled *Sources of Renewal: A Study on the Implementation of Vatican II*, specially prepared for the participants at the forthcoming diocesan synod. The author writes:

> It would be a mistake not to consider the implementation of Vatican II as the response of faith to the word of God as it proceeded from that Council. It is to be hoped that this implementation will be guided by the idea that the renewal which it set on foot is a historical stage in the self-realization of the Church. Through the Council, the Church has not only shown clearly what it thinks of itself, but also in what way it wishes itself to be realized.[5]

It was with this attitude that Cardinal Wojtyła set about implementing tangible measures to facilitate the reception of Vatican II, not just in the Archdiocese of Krakow, but also throughout the whole of Poland. The tools and methods employed to achieve this task were, according to him, the synods, which were not new but were nevertheless effective institutions in the life of the Church. In the years 1971 to 1979, especially at Krakow, one particular circumstance made the diocesan synod well placed, from the pastoral point of view. It was the nine-hundredth anniversary of the death of St. Stanislaus, bishop and martyr, who was killed by the Polish king Boleslaw the Bold, because the bishop reproved him for his immoral behavior. This historical opposition between the pastor and the king must have had various associations within Poland, which was governed by communists, in that the situation in the country was, in many ways (especially religiously), analogous to that in the past.

Cardinal Wojtyła had suggested to the primate of Poland, who held the function of president of the Episcopal Conference in Poland, that he call a plenary synod, which would therefore represent the diocesan synods of the whole country, taking advantage of the aforementioned occurrence. Evidently the primate was not ready for this, because Cardinal Wojtyła turned then to the bishops of the province of Krakow and suggested that they convene the diocesan synods parallel to the Synod of Krakow, or else begin working with the provincial synod, from the fruit of which the dioceses forming part of the Krakow Synod could benefit. Even this proposal did not receive widespread support because three auxiliary bishops did not attend, and consequently the cardinal, in the decree of May 8, 1971, convened the preparatory conference of the Pastoral Synod of the Archdiocese of Krakow at which he entrusted the task of preparing the official inauguration of the Synod within a year, in accordance with his suggestions.

The Diocesan Synod

The commission fulfilled the task it had been set, and pronounced in favor of the pastoral character of the Synod, highlighting that in the course of nine years it would bring about an enrichment of the faith and a fuller formation of Christian attitudes, through "reading the Council," that is, assimilating its doctrines and pastoral orientation, and participating in the whole community's, especially the Catholic laity's, responsibility for the Church. The commission sought to define the structure of the Synod in such a way as to make it possible for the faithful, priests and laypeople, to implement its scope under the current conditions of oppression that made religious life so difficult.

The Synod was run by the bishop ordinary; however, day to day, this task was entrusted to the supporting Central Commission of the Secretariat, the Working Committee, and the Commission of Experts. The composition of the commissions was designated by the bishop. The Central Commission of the Secretariat was responsible for the complexity of the work, for the proposals and their implementation, whether in relation to the content of the documents and the consultation procedure, or for the implementation and functioning of the synodal study groups, which were the Synod's flagship. Diocesan representatives, priests, and religious met in plenary sessions, which initially transmitted information about the progress of the work, but which later took on the task of expressing their support, or lack of it, for adjustments to the documents that were to be presented.

In the work of the Synod, some solutions of primary importance were applied, among which were the study groups. Similarly, the Synod gave considerable attention to every proposal, advice, or critique by the faithful on the behavior of clergy that was contrary to the mission of the Church. Any member of the Church could propose an initiative, suggest problems with which the Synod should concern itself, send drafts of synodal documents, express their opinion on projects put forward by drafting groups, express their ideas publicly, and receive any clarifications they requested. We are only now realizing how the commitment of the Synod of Krakow created at the time an authentic atmosphere of trust and freedom, not only on the religious level within the Church community, but also on the civic level by spreading a sense of responsibility for the common good. Freedom and trust, two values that were absent from totalitarian regimes, and are essential for the growth of the human person, were offered by the Church. The Church desired to help everyone to free themselves from a false ideology and from an inhuman political system, to champion an indispensable religious freedom, and, perhaps even unknowingly, to prepare mankind for a dignified future, by building the foundations of free and democratic conditions for civic and cultural life.

It was not easy to build study groups: in fact, it seemed impossible, in that, on the one hand, the totalitarian system had wiped out ecclesiastical associations once and for all, and had practically eliminated any chance of their emerging in the future, and on the other, any discussion on religious issues, outside of the groups of people that were strictly controlled by the authorities, was impossible. Simply put, the people were afraid to even speak of these issues, even though they could see that it was needed and they had a great desire to do so.

The study groups must have been like the school of the Synod. Directed by priests or by prepared laypeople, they kept the group members informed about the individual conciliar documents, uniting this activity to prayer, the reading of Scripture, and an open discussion that very often followed this pattern: What does the Gospel say about a particular issue? Using the language of the Council, how is this the reality in which we live? And lastly, what should be our response to God on the reality we have found? The first part of the meeting, prayer (contact with the source of revelation and the message of the Council had a catechetical dimension) allowed them to see what God expected of human beings, while the second part of the meeting was to make a comparison of these expectations with human weakness. It is only through this approach that the desire for conversion could arise. Cardinal Wojtyła was adamant about the presence of these elements, even though they could each have different characteristics. The first aspect was what the Church said about the current situation, and then ultimately what we see happening in the future. This formulation brings with it the risk that, out of human weakness, we begin to question God. The situation is tragic, we can't change it: we need then to ask the Church (or God) to modify his requirements and tailor them to human behavior.

At the Synod of Krakow, everyone learned the Council. It was not understood fully either by the members of the Central Commission of the Secretariat, or by the editors of the draft documents, or by any of the other participants. Yet the Synod shone out with unvarnished interior energy, and mobilized many people to put in enormous effort and in study, which engendered a new way of thinking, a new religious consciousness. It was a true spiritual revolution.

Let us not delude ourselves: it did not solve everything. There was, however, undoubtedly a Polish conciliar phenomenon, a pastoral event belonging solely to the Archdiocese of Krakow.

What Happened during the Synod of Krakow and Afterward

The consequences of this pastoral phenomenon were evident especially in the community of the Church of Krakow, but they were not fully accepted in the other dioceses as they practiced the traditional model of synod that was juridical even though they called it pastoral. Nevertheless, the seed of the new method of synodal life had been sown—but it had to die in order to bear fruit. That happened in time, bringing with it the establishment of similar synods in other dioceses, even though not all of them accepted it, until Cardinal Wojtyła became the successor of Peter. A measure of that resistance and of the old mentality that remained was noticeable in the Polish Plenary Synod (1991–99), which obviously lacked the dynamism of the Synod of Krakow.

Contrary to the initial doubts, the study groups grew exponentially. Cardinal Wojtyła expected about fifty to be brought into being, while, to his surprise, almost five hundred were formed. Not all of them were conducted with equal efficiency, but *summa summarum* it was a signal confirmation of the cardinal's pastoral intuition and the discovery of real human needs. Some groups had about a dozen members. Some groups were changed into pastoral councils. The participants of some groups remained in contact with each other still to this day, continuing friendships, collaborating in parish pastoral work.

John Paul II's biographer George Weigel speaks of the positive results of this great operation on Polish society, which was still oppressed. He writes: "Because of the Synod, Krakow experienced neither reactionary movements against the Council, like that of the Lefebvre movement, nor the destruction of the faith and of Catholic practices that accompanied the reception of Vatican II in other cultures and countries."[6]

It would be impossible to analyze all the initiatives and interventions that took place during the nine years of the Synod's activities. The thread that runs through all its work is that they were not dealing so much with documents to study but rather with the capacity to kindle the spiritual life: renewing it, deepening the faith, forming religious attitudes, changing the mentality of the participants. Without doubt, even the final documents, which are the result of prayer, reflection, discussion, and remarkable editorial effort, have their own importance.

It was necessary to ensure that the documents reflected the Synod's conciliar and pastoral character. The thematic key was given by the same Council, above all by the two fundamental constitutions: the Dogmatic Constitution on the Church (*Lumen Gentium*) and the Pastoral Constitution on the Church in the Modern World (*Gaudium et Spes*). The vision of the Church that emerges from them required that we follow their tracks in the documents, showing there the image and role of a particular Church, of the Church of Krakow, which, being a manifestation of the Universal Church, had its own history but which lived in the modern world, in the here and now, and wanted to realize the threefold mission of Christ's salvation (*tria munera*) toward the participation of the whole community of the people of God that constituted the Church of Krakow.

It seemed that this idea, while being the most difficult to implement, in actual fact was a good introduction to the best way to understand Vatican II. To subordinate the issues of the life of faith and pastoral work to the theological categories contained in the *tria munera* is not always easy and clear. What has to be decided is to what point certain aspects of ecclesial life should be associated with the mission, with the prophetic, priestly, or kingly task of the Church.

The first task (*munus propheticum*) means principally eschatological prophecies, the coming of the kingdom of God in the future world. Within the scope of this task, the Synod worked out final documents on announcing the word of the Lord, on developing and passing on the faith in the family, as well as on catechesis, the role of theology in the formation of a life lived through the faith, the ministry of the congregations, and the missionary activity of the Church of Krakow.

The second task (*munus sacerdotale*) highlighted the importance of the sacraments in the life of holiness. This group of documents contained the topics relating to the Eucharist as source and summit of the Christian life, to baptism and confirmation as sacraments that introduce Christian holiness, to reconciliation as the sacrament that allows Christians to participate in Christ's triumph over sin, to the anointing of the sick as the sacrament through which the Christian participates in the sufferings of Christ and in his victory over death, and to holy orders and matrimony as the sacraments of the consecration of time.

The third task (*munus pastorale*) stressed the need to overcome evil. The Synod placed the religious and moral situation of various groups of the faithful under scrutiny: the family, children, young adults, communities committed to charitable works; it underlined the responsibility Christians have to edify the world through culture, professional work, and ecclesiastical structures.

Each document was strictly subdivided into three separate parts: theological, sociological (describing the situation), and pastoral-juridical. The format departed from this structure only in documents that could be considered as appendices. These appendices cover the subjects of ecumenism, the major seminaries for priests, the responsibility of parents, pastoral work concerning the sick, environmental protection, and the responsibility of nations.

Conclusion

The Synod of Krakow, using the means at its disposal, made enormous efforts to revive religious life with that wind of the Holy Spirit that was the Second Vatican Council. First of all, it presented conciliar thought in a highly engaging way, and included both priests and laypeople. Those who had been unable to discuss the problems of the faith in an open, public way for about ten years were given the opportunity to hold that much-needed discussion. This often took the form of a profession of faith that was held up as a valuable witness. The Synod was responsible for uniting priests and laity, allowing the latter to participate in the responsibility not only for the parish, but for the whole Church. Finally, the Synod undoubtedly contributed to a deepening of the faith and of Christian attitudes, which were, when all is said and done, its most important area.

CHRIST AND THE DIGNITY OF THE PERSON

In its penetrating analysis of the modern world, Vatican II reached a point that is particularly important for the visible world: man descending, as Christ did, into the depths of human consciousness, touching the inner mystery of the human person, which in biblical (and also non-biblical) language expresses itself in the word "heart." Christ, the Redeemer of mankind, has penetrated, in a unique and unrepeatable way, into the mystery of the person and has entered the "heart." Rightly, then, Vatican II teaches (*Gaudium et Spes*, n. 22): "In fact, it is only in the mystery of the Word Incarnate that the mystery of the human person finds its light [...]."

JOHN PAUL II, *Redemptor Hominis*, n. 8

THE ORIGINS AND VOCATION OF THE PERSON

ARCHBISHOP IGNAZIO SANNA
Archdiocese of Oristano

Man, Person, and Being

The concept of the human being as person comes principally from the Judeo-Christian tradition of the nature and destiny of man. In fact, the theological truth that man is man insofar as he is a person, constitutes the specific contribution that Christianity, and in particular the Christian conception of man as the image of God, has given to the forming of human identity.

This theological truth is continually being subjected to critical examination by the crucial questions that the human and natural sciences, above all biology, pose. It is impossible to avoid the questions raised by epistemology and the other sciences. One of the ultimate questions that challenge the theological concept of the person, for example, is regarding procreation. So-called procreation is a new science with, as yet, imprecise contours, which arose at the same time that we were beginning to understand the stages through which nature formed a new living being. The obscure world of reproduction lost the holy halo surrounding it and became the subject of interventions ranging from frozen gametes to in vitro fertilization, to the manipulation and conservation of embryos, to the possibility of human cloning. This new science has revealed a new microscopic protagonist, the embryo, the product not of the natural union between two human persons, but of the skillful manipulation of gametes in a laboratory.

In actual fact, there is still no agreement about the definition of what the laboratory-produced embryo *is*—preserved in liquid nitrogen, manipulated in a test tube, and inserted into the uterus that may or may not be different from that of the donor. There is a question about its legal and social status, whether, that is, it is a "person" and has a right to the same protection that would be afforded to the being it will become, or whether it is simply a blob of cells that can be manipulated, experimented on, implanted, or if necessary, discarded when too many have been produced than are required by the couple. The issue about the status of the embryo, where the human person begins and where science's ability to manipulate life should be halted, remains an open question, therefore, at least from the point of view of biological science.[1]

The Christian concept of person that is particularly under discussion, basically, is whether it is enough to be human in order to be a person, or whether you have to be a person in order to be human. The statement of this truth, however, is not immediately clear and unambiguous, because in common parlance the word *person* is synonymous with *human being*. The two terms, *person* and *human being*, are interchangeable and are used to express the same reality, because a person is a human being and not a property of a human being. Even the Italian constitution, which is clearly oriented toward the "person," uses the term according to this generally understood coinage, and states that: "it is the task of the republic to remove economic and social obstacles, which limit the freedom and equality of citizens, [and] also hinder the full development of the human *person*" (section 3). In common parlance, therefore, *human being* is synonymous with *person*. But although everyone agrees on what a human being is, not everyone agrees on what a person is, when a human being begins to be a person, and when he ceases to be one. While the human being is linked to human nature, when taken together with phenomenologically observable and verifiable facts, the person is linked to an interpretation of the living being, borrowed from a religious view of life. The human being is related to life as a biological, determinable, quantifiable, and measurable organism. Person is related to life as *zoe*, as interior dynamism, as charismatic existence, and is not always measurable and quantifiable.

In recent decades, in fact, currents of thought have begun to hold sway by which the equation *human being* = *person* is called into question, because of the fact that not every person could be a human being and not every human being could be a person.[2] The concept of person has been widened to include living beings other than men, insofar as they display a minimum level of consciousness. For moral philosophers H. T. Engelhardt and P. Singer, in deciding whether something has the right to life, what should be taken into account is not its membership in a biological species, but the degree to which it displays self-awareness, the use of reason, and the ability to plan the future.[3]

Singer, particularly, states that the two terms *human life* and *human being* do not coincide. All beings that belong to the species *homo sapiens* have human life, whether it be the fetus that has been conceived by human parents or the "human vegetable" that is irreparably maimed. But even if you could call the latter two "human beings," in reality only those beings that possess the "indicators of humanity" are truly "human," those indicators being self-awareness, self-control, the sense of the future, the sense of the past, the ability to relate to others, regard for others, communication, and curiosity. Only human beings who possess these indicators of humanity are human "persons," says Singer; other human beings who do not exhibit these abilities are part of the human race, but they are not human persons. This means that there can be members of the human species who are not human persons because they do not have the two essential indicators of humanity, which are rationality and self-awareness. The life of these members of the human race, who are not persons, is not sacred, as Christianity, which has imposed this idea on Western civilization, would want it to be. Instead there can be non-human animals who are persons, because they possess self-awareness, like chimpanzees and other animals, while fetuses, newborns, and brain-damaged people are not persons. In conclusion, Singer maintains that membership in the species *homo sapiens* does not authorize a "specist" attitude, with its consequent recognition of particular rights for man.[4]

The extension of the concept of person to the animal kingdom also becomes relevant to the area of robotics. As we know, the reductionist tendencies of robotics maintain that if an entity is capable of rationality, intention, communication, and other prerequisites defined by logic and philosophy, then it is an artificial intelligence that can also have all the attributes of a person. More advanced computers, in fact, can run hospitals, businesses, and military operations, beat chess champions, and manage an impressive amount of information better than human beings. But computers cannot reproduce man's system of thinking. They can deal with information, change it, and can even exhibit behaviors, but only after all these things have been put into the machine by human beings. The computer acts on the basis of input and does so at a very fast rate, which makes it very useful to man. But man who is very much slower, like a tortoise compared with a hare, will always win out in the end. The computer is a machine that acts in a predetermined way; at the very most it can integrate a "random number generator," which can make the machine's behavior unpredictable. But it is not free. Freedom remains the prerogative of the person.[5]

It is worth noting, regarding the broadening of the concept of person, that this was made possible due to the fact that, in contemporary culture, the concept of person has been worked out more from a psychological and ontological point of view, and refers above all to the consciousness that one has of oneself. It is also notable that Karl Barth observes that the twentieth century's change of language has given the concept of person a different meaning from that of the early Church and the Middle Ages, and has reduced it to mean "consciousness of self." He, therefore, while conceding that it is useful to retain the word *person* in Trinitarian theology, if for no other reason than to keep historical continuity, proposes that divine triplicity can be explained by using the term *mode of being*, and that we could therefore say that "God is one in three modes of being, the Father, the Son, and the Spirit." But this great evangelical theologian was very well aware of the limitations of his proposal and admitted:

> We have attempted to find a relatively better response than what is contained in the word "person." The simple fact that we have not been able to do anything other than reiterate the indications suggested by that ancient concept, to gather together under the most fitting idea of a mode of being, should make us perfectly humble and aware of

our limitations. A mere change of terminology is not sufficient to resolve the underlying problems.[6]

Even Rahner says that, after anthropology's input, the concept of person evolved and came to signify a "subject of consciousness."[7]

The Classical Definition of Person

While the concept of person remains semantically and culturally uncertain, we find it necessary, before explaining the authentic meaning of being a person, to put forward a premise in order to recall briefly a few key facts around which nowadays it is possible to find considerable agreement between Christian theologians and philosophers. In the absence of a better definition, Boethius's classical conception of person is still valid, based on an ontological constituent: an "individual substance of rational nature"; or, more simply, according to St. Thomas: a "rational subsistent," "the most perfect thing that exists in nature."[8] The Boethian definition was integrated by Richard of St. Victor in his idea of "ex-sistentia"[9] from the latter's theological reflection, with the necessary addition of the rational dimension. We must not forget, in fact, as Ratzinger observes, that Boethius's concept of person, which has held sway in Western philosophy, has been found wanting when applied to Trinitarian theology and Christology:

> Boethius, remaining within the spirit of Greek thought, defined the person as *naturae rationalis individual substantia*, as the individual substance of a rational nature. As we can see, the concept of person stays completely on the level of substance and cannot be used to explain anything with regard to the Trinity, nor can it be used in Christology; it is an expression that remains on the level of the Greek spirit, which reasons in terms of substance.[10]

Contemporary teaching, when referring to the concept of person, has not penetrated the substance of theological reflection. *Pacem in Terris*, for its part, understands the person as "a nature having intelligence and free will; and therefore subject to rights and duties that spring immediately and simultaneously from its own nature: rights and duties that are, therefore, universal, inviolable, and inalienable" (*Enchiridion Vaticanum*, II, 3, p. 21). The *Compendium of the Social Doctrine of the Church*, in describing nature and the essence of man, does not supply a definition of person, but notes that

> the fundamental message of Sacred Scripture proclaims that the human person is a creature of God (cf. Ps 139:14–18), and sees in his being in the image of God the element that characterizes and distinguishes him (…). [Therefore,] The Church sees in men and women, in every person, the living image of God himself. This image finds, and must always find anew, an ever deeper and fuller unfolding of itself in the mystery of Christ, the Perfect Image of God, the One who reveals God to man and man to himself.[11]

The classical definition of person adopted by the Christian tradition, being predominantly a philosophical/theological one, is not shared universally, and even less by philosophers, doctors, scientists, and lawyers, who have a different view of man and the world, but who, however, profess a philosophical orientation.[12] E. Schockenhoff, criticizing the philosophical neutrality with which many currents in bioethics today join the debate over the concept of person, maintains that

> it is not possible simply to skip the philosophical issues related to the concept of person, without objectively running the risk of applying reductive interpretations to man. Coupled with that is the fact that if we take the point of view of ignoring philosophy while still aware of the problems we always remain locked in a determined philosophical position. A metaphysical concept of person is no different than a merely empirical concept due to the fact that it makes philosophical presuppositions. This is obvious from any point of view we wish to take. The difference lies in the fact that these presuppositions are on the one hand demonstrable and verifiable, and on the other they avoid discussion of those issues by refusing to enter into philosophical controversies.[13]

In today's bioethical language, in which the concept of person does not exist, the most it can do is accept the expression "human individual." The European Bioethics Convention, for example, discussing this issue in January 1995 at the European Council Assembly, could find no agreement on a common definition of person and human being, and it confined itself to affirming as a generally accepted principle that "human dignity must be respected from the beginning of life," and that a "human being is to be understood in the widest sense, both in terms of its individuality and in terms of its membership in the species."[14]

Everyone accepts that there is a conceptual difference between individual and person, in that the semantic scope of individual is much wider than that of person. Books, flowers, cats, and so on, are all individuals, but it is only a person who belongs in some way to the world of the spirit. We could say that every person is an individual, but not that every individual is a person.

It is recognized that a person is such by virtue of what it is and not what it has or does, and also by virtue of the recognition that it can receive from society and from others. Therefore, in order to be a person, it is not necessary that it has developed all its potentialities. If we identified a person according to how it developed and exercised its potentialities, then there would be no theoretical obstacle to allowing abortion, euthanasia, and termination of the mentally retarded and deformed. What must be in place in order to have a person is not its potential but its being.[15] It should be noted, however, that if man's dignity consists in being the person God intended and in being destined for communion with him, "then the existence of every man is legitimized before any inter-human encounter, and this is independent of the degree to which he possesses, or does not possess, the natural signs that distinguish the human being from other creatures."[16]

The Origin of the Concept of the Person

Given this premise, we wish to first clarify further the terms associated with the theological truth we are defending, and then put the concept of person into its proper theological context.

First of all, let us specify that, from an essentially epistemological point of view, the relationship between the concept of person, which possesses human dignity, and the concepts of life and death, cannot be clarified incontrovertibly using the objective criteria provided by the experimental sciences. This kind of relationship has more to do with rights, ethics, and philosophy than science. It is the task of rights and ethics to define when a person can be described as living or dead. The sciences' only task is to supply the methods and principles for defining when living entities already have, or still have, the essential functions of persons. The conceptual analysis of the term *person* is carried out, in fact, with testing that is legal, ethical, and philosophical, not scientific.[17]

For example, if we are trying to ascertain whether a vegetative state is present, science can verify the point at which there is no longer any activity in the cerebral cortex, by using PET scans, electroencephalography, and magnetic resonance. According to science, the cessation of cortical activity, apart from when there is a cardio-circulatory arrest as defined by existing law, does not indicate that the person has died, but that a persistent vegetative state has been established, in which, according to the law, ethics, and philosophy, the essential properties of the person are no longer relevant since they depend upon activity in the cerebral cortex; so also with human dignity. The case of the embryo is analogous. Science is certainly capable of identifying the embryo's stages of growth and the gradual emergence of the most important functions during embryonic, fetal, and newborn life, but it cannot indicate the relationship between the emergence of these functions and the use of the concept of person. The thesis of the emerging person, from the moment an ovum is fertilized by a spermatozoon, is based not on a scientific but on a moral, philosophical, and theological issue of nature. This argument is defended by some philosophers and theologians and contested by others. It is important, however, to observe that, in the case of the embryo, just as in the case of the vegetative state, the divergence lies completely within the area of rights, ethics, faith, and philosophy. These are differences over which scientists have nothing to say from a scientific perspective, and they therefore must remain outsiders.

Second, let us clarify that the anthropology of the human being created in the image and likeness of God, which has led to an ever-clearer perception of its dignity and intangible identity as a person, is in harmony with the development of science, which has placed at our disposal the tools to penetrate the secrets of its natural origin and the biological, psychological, and social dynamics of its existence. The two perspectives, in principle, are not opposed to one another, but need to be articulated without undue dogmatism regarding their points of view. Since the 1600s, the idea of the embryo's delayed animation has prevailed, because of the Aristotelian concept of there being in man an order to the vegetative, sensitive, and intellectual soul. In the eighteenth century, Anton Leeuwenhoek discovered spermatozoa under the microscope, in which he maintained the preformed man was already present. This seemed to constitute the scientific presupposition that at the act of fertilization there already existed, in miniature, the whole man, and therefore animation was immediate. However, by the end of the nineteenth and the beginning of the twentieth centuries, scientific progress came to clarify that it is only when the spermatozoon meets the ovum that a new biological entity was produced, a zygote, genetically distinct from the father and mother, which was open to the possibility of twins, but which in every case, within two weeks, acquired its own individuality. The first cell of every human organism possesses a new genome (informational structure determined by nucleotide sequences of DNA), which gives the organism its genotypical characteristics with an identity that is specific (membership of the human species) and individual (singularity with respect to the parents' organisms and that of other individuals of the same species).

Third, let us clarify that, while affirming that it is not enough to be human beings in order to be persons, we also mean to say that we can describe a human being using different strata, as in psychology, for example. With the human being, we can take into consideration a specific physical constitution or a specific genetic and biological heritage, but with the person, we take into consideration the spiritual and moral potentialities of this particular physical constitution and of this particular genetic and biological heritage. Man, as a living being, can be considered from the purely biological point of view, or from the specifically "human" point of view. In the first case, corresponding with what could be defined as *bios*, we are speaking of a physico-biological phenomenon that can be touched, experienced,

53

measured, and quantified, and that has sexual differentiation as man-woman; in the second case, corresponding with what could be defined as *zoe*, we are speaking of a spiritual reality that we cannot touch or measure or describe quantitatively and that is not differentiated sexually.[18] What does it mean, for example, to say I touch this person? Can a person be touched? (It is interesting that the German language makes the distinction, in order to indicate the same reality, between the term *Körper*, which indicates the physical body of a human being, and *Leib*, which indicates its spiritual reality.) Man exists—because to exist, all that is required is for the organism to work biologically. The person, instead, lives to the extent to which it qualifies the bare existence of the human biological organism with sentiment, decisions, and acts. Animals and plants start and end their cycle of existence without having a perception of the past or the future. The person, instead, lives and moves in a proper sense, carrying out a series of spiritual acts and planning its future on the basis of its past experience. The animal has an "environment" that surrounds it; man has a "world" that he creates himself.[19]

It is clear that in order to avoid misunderstanding, the distinction between human being and person is purely conceptual, not real, and therefore, as such, it cannot be confirmed empirically through facts and external phenomena. The human being is the person and the person is the human being. We cannot split them up, and hence the assertion of J. Eccles: "A being must be considered *human* when its genetic constitution (genotype) is formed from the genetic pool of *homo sapiens*. A human being gradually changes into a *person* through less precise and more debatable means; for example, when it is shown to possess certain social, moral, or intellectual qualities or the reflection of self-consciousness."[20] For the Christian anthropologist, no division exists between body and soul,[21] nor between "corrupt" nature and person "of faith," according to the Lutheran understanding of the phrase. The relationship between individuality and personality is not the same as between an "inferior" nature, in the corporeal and biological sense, and a "superior" nature, in the spiritual and interior sense. Luther had a relational notion of the person, and he drew on this concept for his formulation that the good works of the justified were superseded by justification through God alone. Man is person not by virtue of how he is master of himself, or exists in and of himself, or realizes himself through his works, but insofar as he is a sinner justified by God and freed for merciful love: *fides facit personam*.[22] In Boethius's concentric description, the person appears as the ultimate autonomous bearer of its own qualities. Luther substitutes this with a concept that is radically eccentric, in which the person is not defined on the basis of what it is in itself, but based on what the action of God makes it be. In the Lutheran concept, "the personal being itself is a relational act."[23] God establishes man's personal being, drawing him forth from the reality of sin, made up of a being that is closed in on itself, and opens it to the gift of justification that establishes the person and comes before any action that man may make.

However, we must not forget, on the other hand, as A. Guggemberger writes, that passions, instinctive impulses, and all of sentient life arise from within man as a completely personalized being, and therefore they are specifically human, because they are embraced and fused from within the whole person. All of our highest spiritual acts are nourished from this dynamic. They are qualitatively on a higher level, but they cannot be considered distinct from the vital manifestations of man. They are dependent on nature, because only they can be considered as coming from the person. The bearer and source of all of human life is without doubt the person.[24] For Thomistic anthropology, the duality between soul and body is located on the metaphysical plane of the principles of being: the soul inasmuch as it forms, and the body inasmuch as it is, the raw material. But in the human being, spirit and matter are not divided. The spirit, in man, becomes soul, which is not purely spirit, but is a spirit incarnate, a form of matter. The matter, in man, becomes body, which is not brute matter, but matter informed by the soul. In man, as an incarnate spirit, there is no such thing as a solely spiritual act, detached from sensitivity, from matter. Every spiritual act is also material, and every material act is also spiritual.

The metaphysical unit of soul and body—over and above the Thomistic conception of the soul as a unique substantial form of the body (*De Veritate*, q. 16, a. 1, 13; *Contra Gentiles*, II, c. 69; *De Anima*, a. 14, 11)—is confirmed by the Rahnerian concept of man as incarnate spirit,[25] and by Guardini's notion of consciousness as life.[26] For Guardini, consciousness before it is an intellectual act is an act of

55

life: "Our consciousness is our living."[27] Consciousness is a total act of man in which his sensitivity plays a decisive role. The eye, for example, is "considerably more than an optical instrument which perceives the qualities of color and of form; it is more than a neuro-physical organ transmitting these qualities, in the form of feelings, to the consciousness. The eye sees reality in the form of light; but this means: it sees the essence and the meaning."[28] The world of animate and inanimate material things certainly participates in being, but in it there are only "substantified" things that simply exist; there are some living beings without spirit. Sub-spiritual beings stop before being fully "assimilated into themselves," to which the act of being tends and that renders them possible, inasmuch as *esse est reflexivum sui*. Beings that are capable of consciousness and spiritual love, instead, externalize fully the ability to actualize being, so that they become spiritual existences, persons. "The *materialized* person is the fruit of personalized being."[29]

Fourth, let us clarify that, while affirming that in order to be human beings we must also be persons, man remains by nature man; his "humanity" cannot be unduly extended to non-human beings and needs to be always seen in light of his relationship to God. The Christian faith makes every human being a person and does so not by taking man as a starting point but God. The fact that the various projects started by the new evangelization have attempted to renew the Christian flavor of human society through rebuilding the fabric of the ecclesial community—this face indirectly reveals the anthropological conviction that the Christian is the fully integrated person, and that it is only through throwing open the doors to Christ that one can open the door to every human being. Since man, through the Christian revelation, is created in the image and likeness of God, God is central to our understanding of ourselves. The concept of person in the Christian tradition is primarily in relation to God and relates to man only secondarily and in an analogical way. The Person summons the person; theology summons anthropology. It is this theological dimension of the person that stops man from being considered "from one dimension only," reduced to a purely biological program, to a subject for experimentation and care. Medicine or the biological sciences in general can describe the phenomena of birth and death—they can describe, that is, how one is born or dies—but they have nothing to say about why one is born or dies. For Christians, the why of birth and death, health and sickness, is "revealed," and therefore is part of the faith, before we understand it with our reason. According to neurophysiology, self-aware life is nothing other than a physico-chemical process that is explicable on the basis of ordinary physics and chemistry; mental experience is an aspect of "brain events." But there is no physical or chemical rule, no ideology or philosophy, that can fully explain why one person says to another person, "I love you," thereby revealing the incomprehensible mystery of freedom and human intelligence.[30]

According to work that won a Nobel Prize for medicine, and that goes against the theories of most neuroscientists, the link between mind and brain can be interpreted as an interaction in the cerebral cortex between "psychons" (mental event units) and "dendrons" (material cerebral units), operating on the principles of quantum mechanics. According to the Christian faith, the individual is a person from the beginning of his entirety and completeness, because from the beginning, that is, from always, the individual is shaped by God and "loved by Him" (*Christifideles Laici*, n. 34), regardless of the empirical evidence of human reality. In a way, it is meaningless to ask when an individual begins to be a person and when he ceases to be one.[31] The beginning and the end are lost in the eternal will of God and are outside the historical determination of the human sciences. The beginning and the end are in God. But then, the person is dependent on the eternal mystery of God, while the individual belongs to freedom and to history.[32]

The truest origin of the concept of person, therefore, is theological even if, on the one hand, there is a confused idea of this already in ancient classical literature,[33] and even if, on the other, this theological origin has been lost over the centuries and the concept of person progressively secularized, such that it has become the prerogative of philosophy and law.[34] From the divine Person we pass to the human person, from theology to philosophy and law, in a sort of circular movement where anthropology and theology are intertwined reciprocally.[35]

It is true that the anthropological bent of St. Augustine in his Trinitarian theology introduced the principle of analyzing the depths of the human spirit in order to discover there an access route to representing the image of the Trinity. But if it is true that the image of the individual's spiritual life helped the Christian mind to understand the mystery of the tripersonal God, the revelation of this mystery, fulfilled in Christ, has also been of considerable help to us in understanding ourselves as persons. This means that in order to understand the human being's personal being, it is necessary to begin with the personal being of God, because the experience of God is more decisive for understanding the nature of mankind than is the experience of mankind for understanding the nature of the Triune God.[36]

St. Thomas's assertion can be understood in this sense, by which the meaning of the name *person* belongs more primarily and appropriately to God than to his creatures. Of itself, the name can refer to the latter only in an analogical sense. If we consider, however, the significance attached to something and the way in which we attach a name to something, then the term *person* is more convenient for creatures.[37] J. Galot points out, quite correctly in this regard, that

> the principle of analogy, accepted in the domain of nature, is equally applicable in the order of persons. If man has been created in the image and likeness of God, then his person as well as his nature bear a reflection of what exists in God. So we cannot claim that the human person must be defined in completely different terms from the divine person. According to the fundamental analogy, if, in God, what constitutes person is relation, then we must expect that relation likewise formally constitutes the human person (…). True, this intellectual process follows the analogy by an upward process. We raise our sights from man to God. Now, on the contrary, we are proceeding in the opposite direction. From what is said about the divine persons in Trinitarian doctrine we come back down to the level of the human person. But the legitimacy of the ascending analogy guarantees the legitimacy of the descending analogy.[38]

The Theological Dimension of the Person

In wishing to determine, then, what the constitutive dimensions of the person are—that is, what makes every human being a human being—we need to begin with the theological dimension, which is fundamental, in order that through the necessary mediation of Christ, we may reach the anthropological dimension, which is derivative and analogical. It is the theological dimension that is the basis for and protects the uniqueness of every human being, which makes a human being a person, a conduit of God, the only creature that God has willed for itself (*Gaudium et Spes*, n. 24).[39] As John Paul II writes, "The most radical and elevating affirmation of the value of every human being was made by the Son of God in his becoming man in the womb of a woman" (*Christifideles Laici*, n. 37).

Now, under this theological origin of the concept of person, the human being understands himself as a spiritual being endowed with eternal values, able to enter into dialogue with a transcendent God. When God creates a human being, he does not create just another object among other objects, but he creates a "you," calling it by name (Isa 43:1: *I have called you by name, you are mine*), placing it before him as a responsible being, a being, that is, that can respond, a partner in interpersonal dialogue.[40] If, as in the current theology of creation, creation is subordinated to this union and we maintain that the creation of the world and of mankind is the presupposition of the historical union between God and mankind,[41] we are indirectly saying that everything that exists has been created for mankind. Humanity is the "crown" of the world, not in the sense of an embellishment, but in the sense that all creation has been designed for it. Without humanity, the Earth is, as it were, waiting in a state of incompleteness. God brought to a conclusion the work he had done (Gen 3:19) only after mankind's creation, in such a way that the human being does not exist without his world and the world does not exist without the human being. But humanity is not just earth, matter. God infuses humanity with the breath of life, that is, the light of self-knowledge, as the breath of life is defined (Prov 20:27), so that the human being becomes a living being, a person. Although he is part of the earth and, therefore, essentially tied to it, the individual is open to God, who makes him live and gives him his precise personal identity. By saying that mankind is part of the earth, what we mean is that mankind belongs to the world and the world belongs to mankind, in that it is a world that comes forth and manifests itself fully in mankind.

In the light of this reality, therefore, the true essence of humanity is not that of being a microcosm, a little world, claiming the world as an anthropological point of reference, but that of being created in the image of God. For Plato, the earthly image of the divine was not one human being, but the cosmos in all its complexity.[42] For Christian faith, instead, the image of the divine is one individual, who is a little god. His anthropological point of reference is God. God is the human being's "you," just as the human being is God's "you." It is God who *speaks* mankind, and what constitutes the bedrock of his dignity is being called to live and act as the "you" of God. Mankind is the image of God and, as such, is directed toward God, and it is only with God that he can be true man. The human being, as the conciliar doctrine *Gaudium et Spes* says, is conceptually and existentially illuminated by the mystery of the Word Incarnate (see n. 22). The God of Jesus Christ, the Triune God is the principal and, in a certain sense, the only source of every anthropological statement.[43] John Paul II observed that "while the various currents of human thought both in the past and at the present have tended and still tend to separate theocentrism and anthropocentrism, and even to set them in opposition to each other, the Church, following Christ, seeks to link them up in human history, in a deep and organic way."[44] The separation between God and humanity, writes D. Mongillo, the opposition between theocentrism and anthropocentrism condemns the human being to radical misunderstanding. Their union is the nucleus of the anthropological mystery seen in the light of Jesus Christ. In him, God and the human being constitute one and the same mystery. Anthropologies without theology miss the problem of the supreme dimension of the human condition. Theologies without anthropology distort and disfigure the mystery of God. According to the Christian message, theology is anthropology and anthropology is theology: God and humanity cannot be thought of separately.[45]

Therefore, we distort the deepest reality of the human being if we want to consider it only from below, from its relationship with the world of nature and the animal kingdom. The individual is a priori a being that is answerable to God and created by him, and on the basis of this divine likeness, which is his true dignity, he is fundamentally different from all subhuman things.[46] His dignity, however, is not an absolute thing and is not dependent on some quality of value that the individual has in himself, like his soul, his intelligence, his virtue. It is something relative to God, because it derives from the human being by virtue of the fact that he is a manifestation and revelation of God in a role that is above all of visible creation. While other things exist only through a dependent causal relationship to God, and thereby fully manifest their power, not just their nature, the human being is a reflection of the mystery of God himself and in the deepest essence of his spirit makes visible who God is, that is, pure person in perfect love and freedom. The human being is the only place in the visible world where God is recognizable as personal spirit, because he points the way to God not just by existing, but also by being a personal spirit. The relative autonomy of the human spirit, like God, is a higher form of the natural revelation of God, even if always in an obscure, hidden, and inadequate way.

Every individual and all human beings are unique and unrepeatable; every individual is a value in and of himself. The fact that God created man for himself, as end and not means, makes him an absolute value, which cannot be made operational in any reality, whether production, class, state, religion, or society.[47] The human being as person is an absolute value, because God considers him in an absolute way. Christ, a man among men, through his life and his work of redemption has confirmed the absolute value of the human person, because he died for *every* individual, for *every* brother and sister (1 Cor 8:11; 1 Tim 2:5–6). According to E. Schockenhoff, the baptismal liturgy of the Church, adopting the rite of anointing of kings and anointing the baptized with chrism, expresses the conviction that before God every individual is valued as a king. The fact that this likeness to God, then, is recognized independently of social or religious position and is not tied to any other condition is a powerful witness to the value of every individual human life.[48] A passage in the *Talmud*, referred to by the moral theologian of Regensburg, attributes the value of the whole world to man, as if to state that human life—contrary to the lapidary opinion of Caiaphas (*it was better to have one person die for the people*; John 18:14)—is not in principle quantifiable and is not open to any utilitarian worldly interpretation: "Adam was created as an incomparable individual to teach us that if one destroys a person it should be treated as if one had destroyed a whole world, and to teach us that if one keeps a person alive it should be treated as if one were keeping the whole world alive."[49] According to a rabbinical tradition, God would have prohibited man from making images of him, because he has made his own image in creating man.

The Christological Dimension of the Person

If it is true that the first and fundamental dimension of the person is theological, and that it is dependent on the transcendence of God, it is also true, however, that God's transcendence reveals itself to us through the historical event of Christ. In order to deal with both the transcendence of God and the proximity of human beings, it is necessary to meditate on Christ. Therefore, the person has a Christological dimension, whether we wish to define it by its relationship to God or by its relationship to other human beings. Above all, Christ helps us to understand himself as a person. However, in order to express ourselves in a theologically correct and human way, and in a way that reveals the Christological dimension of the human person, it is necessary first to free ourselves from some misunderstandings that the concept of person has suffered from in Western thought. The first of these misunderstandings, according to J. Ratzinger, lies in asserting that Christ lacks complete humanity, because, since he is the Son of God, he has only a divine person, but not a human person. The Christological dogma that we profess affirms that in Christ we find the one divine person, but with two natures, human and divine. But the concept of person used here has almost always been thought of in terms of substance, according to Greek and Latin categories that are understood on the level of essence, and not in existential terms, according to proper theological categories that are seen on the level of existence. The second misunderstanding consists in "the idea that Christ is the unique ontological exception" and, therefore, should be treated as an exception to the rules, not able to be expressed according to common conceptual schemes.[50] Another way of saying this: because the divine person of Jesus Christ is an exception within all of humanity's history, he cannot be considered as the norm for man's human person.

We can clear the field of these misunderstandings if we reflect on the fact that, according to the Second Council of Constantinople (553), with regard to the Incarnation, the "person" of the Son is a "compound" person: "The holy Church of God (...) confesses the union of the Word of God with flesh by composition, that is by hypostasis. This union by composition not only preserves the mystery of Christ without confusing the elements that come together in unity, but does not permit their separation" (Denzinger 425). This description of the human-divine reality of Jesus as a "compound person" leads us to say that his divine person was in some way "humanized," and that, in an authentically human way, it lived out his historical, individual, and social existence. Christ's being a divine person did not empty his human being, but brought it to the greatest level of personalization, that is, to the maximum level of consciousness and freedom. Briefly, we can maintain that the individual's being a person reaches its completion in the humanization of the person of the Word by the Incarnation.[51] According to J. Ratzinger:

> in Christ, who is certainly presented by the faith as a unique case, we are not dealing only with a speculative exception, but one that shows itself truly as what we mean by the enigma of man. Scripture expresses this by calling Christ the last Adam or the "second man." Christ has become the revelation of the whole essence of man, such that the Christological concept of person constitutes an indication of how one should interpret the person itself (cf. *Gaudium et Spes*, 22).[52]

The person of Christ is the person who, in the Spirit, gathers all unto himself, and reconciles us to God and each other.

Jesus Christ, being Son, is unique and without equal, because only he has a relationship with the Father that is constituted in his personal existence. But in his resurrection, he has given the believer his Spirit, the same life-giving principle of his own existence, in virtue of which he has brought to its end his historical existence; the same Spirit whose power raised him from the dead. In this way, Jesus has become the principle of new life for all men. By being man, he has become a paradigm for all men. Because of the Holy Spirit coming to us as the Spirit of Jesus, we can all participate in his divine sonship, which only he possesses from his origin. The principle of our existence is the same one that animates that of Jesus. Just as in Jesus the hypostatic union does not mean a diminishing of or detraction from his humanity but its greatest fulfillment, so also in the believer the presence of the Spirit that reproduces the image of Jesus implies the greatest perfection of his personal being. If Jesus is person through his relationship to the Father, then the believer also is person to the extent to which he or she is called to participate in that relationship, although always on the basis of his or her nature as a creature. The Spirit of Jesus, present within him, makes openness to God possible, and makes his essential relationship to God possible, and so contributes to the realization of human perfection. Greater union with God means, in fact, that a greater realization of that creaturely essence and being is possible.[53]

Christ helps the human being to save himself as a person. Christology has given a notable contribution to anthropology, not only with regard to understanding the human being, but also with regard to his salvation as person. It has redefined human identity, because it interprets it in the light of Christ's existence. We could even say that Christ saves each human being, because it leads to his most authentic perfection as person.[54] In fact, in fundamental Christian anthropology, in order to be a person, it is not enough simply to be a human being, but it is necessary to be integrated with Christ. It is true that there is no reference to the relationship with Christ in the definition of person that tradition has handed down to us. But in the order of the story of salvation, the human being has been designed from the beginning as a person, because he is created in Christ, the perfect image of God. The human being is not, therefore, simply a being open to the transcendence of the mystery of God, but is above all a Christ-centered being, because he is historically defined as a person through his relationship to Christ.[55]

Now, being a person in Christ is not just an initial fact, but also a vocation, a task to be fulfilled:

Created as person in Christ, the human being is called to live out his relationship with Him, through the interpersonal nature of his existence, to reach his destiny of perfect union with Him. This involves a process of personalization lived consciously and freely through the encounter with Christ, in faith, in the Church community, in order to realize the fulfillment of his filial person according to the plan of God.[56]

The human being, therefore, precisely because he is created in Christ, his perfect image, aspires to personalize himself. The original dignity of the human being is, therefore, that of *being* a person in Christ. The existential task and fundamental vocation of each human being is to become a person in Christ. In fact, the human being, from the moment of birth, is defined by his genetic code, which is integrated into a specific reality, and by its cultural code, which is integrated into a specific history. From birth, the human being lives out his individual destiny, and exists, that is, as a being tending toward a condition of free existence. But Christ is the savior of each individual, because he leads him to realize his vocation of being a person through a second birth from on high. It is from this second birth "from on high," that the human being, through Christ, can realize his vocation to be person in an authentic existence of freedom in the Spirit (John 3:17).

Christ does not claim the title savior because he brings to the world a beautiful revelation or an elevated teaching on the person, but because he introduces into humanity's history the true reality of the person for the whole man.[57] The human being, therefore, is created from the beginning in the true condition of "person," in love and in freedom, and sharing God's own mode of being. When he then becomes a person in Christ, he realizes the relationship between his being in itself and other persons: the relationship of communion. In Christ, the human being can affirm his existence as person, not because of the inviolable laws of nature, but by grounding himself in a relationship with God, identical to the relationship Christ has, as Son, with the Father, freely and in love.[58] In other words, Christology offers mankind the opportunity to raise the condition of the human individual and person. Modern culture has separated the concept of person from its religious origin and transformed it into tragic individualism, nihilism, and death.[59] The sociologist F. Alberoni has admitted in the *Corriere della Sera* [an Italian newspaper—ed.] that one of the greatest omissions of our age has been the loss of the metaphysical sense of the person: the understanding that every human being has something of the divine—a value and a mystery. It is in Christ that every human being "can affirm his existence as person, not because of the inviolable laws of nature, but grounding himself in a relationship with God, identical to the relationship Christ has, as Son, with the Father, freely and in love."[60]

It is clear that in explaining the theological and Christological dimension as part of the makeup of the person we do not intend to circumscribe the ability of believers to recognize themselves and others as personal individuals and absolute values. Even secular humanists can and must give an account of their affirmation that each individual is an end in itself. Human reason can demonstrate that the human being is an intelligent and free being, and therefore, by nature, spiritual—and, as such, an end in itself.[61] Think of how Kant insisted on how the person should not be manipulated in relation to other human beings and society. From the principle that rational nature exists as an end in itself, the philosopher of Konigsberg obtained the categorical imperative that one should always act in such a way as to always treat humanity, whether in its own person or in the person of another, as an end and never simply as a means.[62] However, what we must recognize in the first place is that, when we attribute an absolute value to a human being, we indirectly acknowledge the existence of an Absolute as the basis of this person's respect and dignity. In reality, outside of a religious vision that sees in the human being at least a distant presence of God, it is very difficult to establish why the human being's dignity is absolute and therefore intangible. John Paul II states that the sense of man is directly linked to the sense of God, and maintains that

> the Gospel of God's love for man, the Gospel of the dignity of the person and the Gospel of life are a single and indivisible Gospel (…). [On the other hand,] in the midst of difficulties and uncertainties, every man who is sincerely open to the truth and to the good, in the light of reason and with the secret inpouring of grace, can discover in the natural law written on the heart (Rom 2:14–15) the sacred value of human life from beginning to end and can claim

the right of every human being to have this respected as its primary good.[63]

However, we need to recognize that, from a historical point of view,

it is only in the Christian doctrine of God's incarnation in humanity that we find explained and brought to its natural conclusion the humanist intuition that the human being is the supreme being for humanity, stating with unequaled effectiveness the ethical imperative of human relations based on the personal dignity of each individual, and decisively opposing a relational model where nature prevails upon the person, where we turn others into things, and where abstract entities (the state, race, society, class) become the mediators of real individuals; where, in short, we never truly begin to understand that each human being must be treated like God, because God has wanted to be a human being, and to allow us to treat him as such.[64]

The Anthropological Dimension of the Person

From the Christian concept of the human being created in the image and likeness of God and integrated into Christ, we derive in some way the essential anthropological dimension of the person, which can be grouped and summarized into *subsistence* and *self-transcendence*.[65]

With regard to *subsistence*, the human being exists in himself as a unique and unrepeatable being, exists as an "I," able to turn in on himself, understand himself, possess himself, choose for himself. In fact, to *subsist*, for the person, means to exist of himself (*a se*), in himself (*in se*), and for himself (*per se*). Aseity, or existing of oneself, means that a person is an autonomous being, free to decide. Inseity, or existing in oneself, means that the person is an intelligent and conscious being in that it is able to turn in on itself, to reflect on itself, and to have consciousness of itself and of its acts. Perseity, or being for oneself, means that the person is its own end and cannot be used as a means. In this way, the subsistence that defines the person is the existence of a spiritual substance, because only the spirit is intelligent and therefore has a conscience and has freedom. In other words, to subsist is "to exist as I," that is, as the capacity to turn in on oneself (*esse est reflexivum sui*) and, therefore, to understand oneself and possess oneself and consequently determine oneself. However, it is not intelligence, conscience, and freedom that define the person: it is the person, inasmuch as it is a subsistent being, that is the source of all acts of intelligence, conscience, and freedom. These acts can also be lacking, and without them the human being ceases to be a person.[66]

With regard to *self-transcendence*, the human being is open to the infinite and to all created beings. Above all, he is open to the infinite, that is God, because through his intellect and his will, he raises himself above all of creation and himself, he makes himself independent of other creatures, he is free of other creatures, and he tends toward the whole truth and the absolute good. He is also open toward others, other human beings and the world, because it is only when he can use "you" as a reference point that he can say "I." He comes out of himself, from the egotistical desire to preserve his own life, and he enters into a relationship of dialogue and communion with others.[67] According to St. Thomas, the person is open to the totality of being, to the limitless horizon of being, and has within himself the capacity to transcend the individual objects that he knows, in fact, through his openness to being without limits. The human soul is, in a cognitive sense, all things: "all immaterial things enjoy a certain infinity, in that they embrace everything, either because they are in essence a spiritual reality that serves as a model and likeness of everything, as in the case of God, or because they operate like angels, or have the potential to, like souls."[68] The movement of the *exitus* toward the infinite and toward the outside world is also at the same time the movement of the *reditus* toward themselves. The human being returns from the outside world to himself and by doing so shows his subsistence, because *redire in se ipsum* is synonymous with subsisting.[69]

For M. Buber, a modern anthropological reflection deals with not only the relationship between "I" and "things" that delimit the field of human experience, but above all with the relationship of the "I" with the "you" that drives the person to encounter and immerses it fully in the dynamism of dialogue. The I-you relationship is not something accidental or superfluous added to the person, but the interpersonal space that reveals and constitutes the "I as I" and the "you as you," in a horizon of equality, openness, and availability for communion.[70] According to John Paul II, being a person means to tend toward self-realization, which cannot be achieved without "a sincere gift of self." The model for such an interpretation of the person is God himself as the Trinity, as a communion of Persons. To say that we are created in the image and likeness of this God means also that we are called to exist "through" others, to become a gift.[71]

The person, therefore, is "being-within-itself" (*esse in*), an "I," through its substance. Through its self-transcendence, it is a "*being-for-others*," a relational being (*esse ad*), and a being in communion with God and with other human beings. It is at the same time a potency of infinity and a potency of communion. Both of these two potencies that characterize the human person find their greatest realization in God, supreme being and infinite love, for whom we could say that the human being is person only to the extent that he is the image of the supreme being and the infinite love of God.

VERUM BONUM IN THE MORAL TEACHING OF JOHN PAUL II

PROF. WOJCIECH GIERTYCH, OP
Theologian of the Pontifical Household

Introduction

Liberty in the Holy Spirit is a central theme in the mind of St. Paul, who after being blessed by an encounter with Jesus on the road to Damascus recognized how enslaving his previous religiosity had been. To the Galatians he wrote: "When Christ freed us, he meant us to remain free. Stand firm, therefore, and do not submit again to the yoke of slavery" (Gal 5:1). The location of this major assertion within the entire Christian message and within its moral teaching—which involves a clarification of the relationship of grace to nature and of the possibility of God working within the human will in such a way that the human will becomes not less but more free, in accord with the Pauline statement that "it is God, for his own loving purpose, who puts the will and action in you" (Phil 2:13)—is the central challenge that is facing twentieth-century Catholic moral theology. It is not sufficient that liberty in the Spirit will be announced in the kerygma of teaching. It needs to be spelled out within a clear and practical description of the psychic and moral transformation of the person engineered by divine grace, and it needs to be clearly differentiated from such an understanding of liberty that sees itself entitled to be divorced from the objectivity of the real, of inherent finalities, of the other and his or her dignity, and from the objectivity of anything that can offer human life a lasting and true meaning and deepest happiness.

When Karol Wojtyła attended the Second Vatican Council and when he embarked upon his major philosophical works such as *Osoba i czyn* [*The Acting Person*] and *Miłosc i odpowiedzialność* [*Love and Responsibility*], it was abundantly clear that the Marxist experiment of human liberation had failed. The new anthropology that was to liberate man from the challenges of a free economy, from the enslaving shackles of traditional religious and moral values, and from a rooting in a national and cultural identity, had instead locked not only individuals but also entire nations in a vast political and economic machine in which the individual was reduced to the rank of a mere cog with no field for personal and social responsibility, no personal creativity and maturity, no room for individual growth, no right to personally perceive and adhere to truth and goodness. Hence, Wojtyła's profound philosophical analysis of the interior springs of human action, that is, of human subjectivity, was geared toward the liberation of the person from within. This intellectual project was born within the social *Sitz im Leben* of a Marxist dictatorship, but its focus extended far beyond that context. It continues to have deep implications for the renewal of Catholic moral theology, including in those places where totalitarian dictatorships are unknown, but where the ideologies of moral laissez-faire liberalism, under the umbrella of the dictatorship of relativism, and of hedonist nihilism thrive, proposing a variant of liberty that does not contribute to the maturity of personal subjectivity but enslaves the human spirit, not so much by external social, political, or religious forces, but by the even more pernicious internal forces of an immature, disorganized, and chaotic psyche.

The Pauline theme of spiritual liberation has not been absent in modern Catholic theology, but it certainly has been overshadowed in the moral instruction that was given through the casuist-centered manuals of moral theology of the modern centuries. The incisive development of moral reflection in medieval thought—which had been built on the spiritual perspective of the Fathers of the Church, searching for the divine image, the icon of Christ, painted within the moral endeavors of the individual as he built up his own interior ethical structure founded upon the supernatural organism of grace and the personal virtues, both theological and moral, moved by the inspiration of the Holy Spirit, and leading to the promised beatitude—

71

was superseded in modern traditional moral theology by a vision reduced basically to an almost Pelagian obedience of the conscience to the externally imposed and having a voluntarist connotation of the commandments. This obligation-centered vision of morals was strengthened further by the philosophy of Kant with its focus on the obligatory and its mistrust of happiness, understood to be an egoist eudaemonism.

Karol Wojtyła's Input into the Second Vatican Council

The approach that reigned in Catholic moral theology before Vatican II generated dissatisfaction, but serious studies in this field prior to the Council were lacking. For this reason, Vatican II did not give us a specific document on moral theology. Among the drafts prepared for the Council was the *Constitutio de ordine morali christiano*, which in a negative way emphasized the dangers that assail Catholic morality, such as subjectivism and situational ethics. This document contrasted these dangers with the objective and absolute moral order, presented as a two-level morality (natural and supernatural, general and elitist), suggesting the extraordinary nature of the spiritual life. The projected constitution expressed doubts about the primacy of charity in moral life, fearing that charity may change into verbalism and sentimentalism at the expense of the commandments. It stressed primarily the moral order, which was seen to have its source in the will of God. Moral law was interpreted as a manifestation of the divine will, which imposes an obligation, and not as an expression of divine wisdom addressed to human reason and liberty. The central issue seemed to be not the cognition of truth, but obedience to rules, which can be unjustified. There was hardly any mention of grace, of the evangelical message, of Scripture. The almost unique reference to natural law gave the draft a Stoic and not a Christian bias, with virtues seen as models to be followed and not as capacities infused in the soul by grace.

Even though during the Council, the projected constitution was subjected to numerous amendments, it was finally rejected and the Council did not produce a new version in its place. However, a fragment of the draft of the constitution found a place in the conciliar decree *Inter Mirifica*, in which "the Council declares the primacy of the objective moral order that is to be upheld without reserve by all."[1] Yet, the question how moral issues were to be addressed could not be ignored, and so it reappeared again during the preparation of *Gaudium et Spes* on the Church's place in the modern world. The preparatory commissions once more were perplexed as to how to present moral issues.

As Archbishop Pierre d'Ornellas has shown in his major study on the contribution of Karol Wojtyła to Vatican II, it was in this moment that the young bishop from Krakow presented his own proposition of resolving the dilemma.[2] Coming from his experience of living in a communist regime, Wojtyła centered his reflection on liberty. He saw that it is not the will of God imposing a moral order from without that is to be in the center of a theological anthropology, but the liberty of the individual who freely adheres to the true good. The perception of the place of the Church in the world may commence, therefore, with the human person, his spiritual faculties, his capacity for the cognition of truth, and his free attachment to moral goodness. The objectivity of the moral order does not have to be seen uniquely through an external moral law, but also may be seen through the fact that the human person strives toward the "true good."

It was in this moment that the phrase *verum bonum*, the "true good," appeared in the conciliar debates. The conscience that is focused on the *verum bonum* has its dignity, even when it is erroneous, and so it must be respected and, of course, formed. Education, which supplies arguments, assists the conscience in perceiving the true good. The cognition of the true good, therefore, precedes liberty and is its foundation. This approach stressed that it is through the judgment of the conscience of individuals that the Church is primarily present in the world (more so than through concordats, constitutions of states, coronations of kings, and so on), and that this judgment of the conscience deserves to be respected both by the civil authorities and by the Church.

Wojtyła's text defended the objectivity of the moral order, but in a different way from that of the earlier projected constitution *de ordine morali*. His intuition was followed up and developed in

Gaudium et Spes. The Council showed the observation point from which the presence of the Church in the world is to be perceived. That observation point is the human person, capable of discerning the true good, and capable of responding to it through a personal gift of self. While Wojtyła's reflection of this issue was primarily philosophical, the Council located this intuition in a Christological setting. It is Christ in his total gift of self who manifests the supreme possibilities of graced humanity. In union with his grace, the spiritual faculties of reason and the will can be purified, strengthening their capacity to perceive the *verum bonum* and to adhere to it. Toward the end of the Council, in the light of subsequent debates, it was clear that the objective moral order does not flow uniquely from an externally imposed source, but finds its essential meaning within the creative action of the acting person. Liberty, reason, conscience, truth, and the moral law are rooted not only in an externally imposed moral order, but above all in the human person, which has its dignity as a child of God, renewed by grace. A theological anthropology built on the study of Christ's humanity can therefore correct moral theology, ensuring that the individual's drive for the *verum bonum* will be central in his life.

Verum Bonum in the Philosophical Research of Wojtyła

In the years just before Vatican II, Karol Wojtyła, the professor of ethics at the Catholic University of Lublin, had studied deeply the theme of the *verum bonum*. His research centered upon the position of Aquinas, but he viewed the medieval doctrine in the light of the input of modern philosophers, even though in his conclusions he attributed prime value to the former's philosophical synthesis. The comparison of Aquinas's presentation of the *verum bonum* within the moral act with other schools of thinking clearly manifests Wojtyła's conviction that eliciting the individual's capacity for adherence to the true good is not a simple affair. It can be subject to distortions due to erroneous opinions about the nature of the moral act, and that is why it needs a careful moral education. As the years passed, Wojtyła reached the conclusion that Aquinas's metaphysical vision could profit from the enrichment of a phenomenological and experimental perspective attentive to the level of the individual's experience, but the perspective of modern philosophers still urgently needed the backing of the clear principles of Aquinas's metaphysical ontology. The fact that the Aristotelian and Thomistic philosophy of being makes use of analogous concepts is, as Wojtyła asserted, no cause for their rejection, because it is through such concepts that a correct understanding of reality may be attained.[3]

Following Aquinas, Wojtyła noted that the two spiritual faculties of reason and the will function together, with reason perceiving the truth about the good that is the object of the will. The will wills the reason to know. Reason knows that the will wills and it knows the object of the will's willing. As a result, truth and goodness are intermingled. The good that is the object of the will becomes a truth as it is perceived by reason. This truth may have a theoretical meaning when it is known in itself or a practical meaning when it is geared to action. As reason perceives the good, it perceives distinctions within that good, in particular the basic distinction between the honest, the useful, and the delightful good. When the will moves to the good for itself, that good is desired as an honest good. When that good is desired in view of something else, it is desired as a useful good. Both these goods are to be distinguished from the delightful good, which is a purely subjective good granting the subject some form of pleasure or delight. The value of the useful good depends then on whether it is tied to the honest or to the merely delightful good. Since it is reason that ascertains the good in itself in its correspondence with the dignity of human nature, perceiving that it is a good that can be desired by the will in an honest way, the reason enjoys a certain supremacy.[4] Reason can perceive the honesty of the good because, as Wojtyła noted in his 1956 to 57 lectures, "the honest good bears within itself the 'splendour' of reason; it has within itself its ontic perfection and this causes the reason to base itself on it in its normative activity, so that as a good it determines then about the specifics of the rational being."[5] The reason, since it perceives the hidden splendor within the good, can then direct the entire human person in its moral life and objective development.

Wojtyła described the perception of the truth about the good as a normative process. Being able to perceive rationally the essence of goodness in a general manner, reason acquires a capacity to formulate a norm. Other beings such as animals also strive for various goods, sometimes even for the same goods that man strives for, but man is the only being capable of grasping the general essence of goodness—the *communem rationem boni*—and of then willing it as such. Thus the relationship of man to various goods is permeated by a norm. This norm is not something that is imposed from without, but is formulated by reason itself in its perception of goodness under the ratio of the general good. This formulation of norms takes place in the form of judgments, in which always appears the general concept of the good that the reason of the acting subject is capable of perceiving in its truth. That judgment about the truth, then, is the source of the moral norm for the acting subject. The subject is the author only of the judgment about truth, not of the truth itself, which he only reveals, thereby tying, that is, obliging, his liberty by that truth. Within the scope of man's intellectual vision, as he profits from the general concept of the good, a hierarchy of goods may appear. That the reason can assess their measure is ultimately due to the fact that reason understands the essence of the good. This recognition of this essence is not the fruit of a Platonic contemplation of the idea of goodness in itself, but it is the result of the abstracting of the general good from particular goods done by reason itself.[6] That general good perceived by reason is always perceived as a truth, because truth is always the basic object of reason, even as it views the proper object of the will.

Since the will is a rational appetite in its essence, and not only due to an external participation in the rationality of the reason, it inherently needs the supportive light of reason in its adherence to the good. It can therefore be said that reason has a normative role in respect to the will, even though both faculties function together. Ethical acts of the will are such that they suppose the normative acts of the reason. Such acts of the will that act against the norm of reason are therefore morally evil.[7] These acts, however, are not just errors of reason, because they involve not only reason but also the will, which is active. In the act of choice, there is not only the moving toward one value with the simultaneous eschewing of other values (which would be a purely "material" understanding of choice). Choice also involves above all the determination about the objects presented in an intentional way to the will on the basis of the certitude of truth. This determination is the fruit of both the will and the reason. The reason supplying the perception of truth is therefore necessary in every act of the will, but its presence is most clearly evident in an act of choice.[8]

Moral life therefore consists in the striving for the truth of the matter within human behavior. Man "experiences" the truth about the good within the moral act, and he undertakes the good in the act as it is subjected to the criterion of reason, that is, within the light of the truth. In the essence and structure of every human act that is undertaken consciously and freely, there is therefore involved the formulation of a norm by the individual's reason. The individual "experiences" this formulation of the norm as an essential and constitutive element of his moral acts. This experience is a reflex of the consciousness that accompanies these acts, and it mirrors that which is happening within the reason and will. The life of these spiritual faculties is centered therefore on the truth about the good.[9]

In his philosophical essays and lectures, Karol Wojtyła compared the Thomistic understanding of the moral act with the understanding of other schools of thought of modernity. He showed that David Hume's understanding of the role of reason within the moral act reduced it to a merely ancillary role, because Hume focused uniquely on the useful good, giving up the attempt to specify an end that would correspond with the rational nature of man and would be an honest good. Opposing the position of those who recognized as virtuous only those who follow reason in their acts, Hume declared that reason itself can never be the motive for any act of the will and that it can never oppose the emotions as they direct the will. Hume restricted the functioning of the reason to the issuing of strictly precise proofs and to the contemplation of the separate relationships between ideas, divorcing reason from the will that introduces it into the world of real beings. The reason can only inform about causes and effects, about what can elicit pleasure or displeasure, and so it can function only in an ancillary manner without having the capacity to direct moral acts. Wojtyła quoted Hume's statement that "reason is, and ought only to be, the slave of the *passiones*, and can never pretend to any other office than to serve and obey them."[10] What, therefore, for Aquinas was a base action beneath the nature and dignity of reason, for Hume was natural, this being a consequence of his empiricist assumptions. Hume associated morality with feelings rather than with judgments even though these feelings can sometimes be so subtle that we are inclined to interpret them as ideas. This, however, Hume claimed to be a misinterpretation because reason has no influence upon the emotions and the will.[11] Since it is an emotional moral sense rather than reason that offers some moral guidance, for Hume normative sentences were pointless. Reason, not having any directive and normative function, can only limit itself to the description of the moral sense. This led to utilitarianism, to such a use of reason that would maximize pleasure.

Since in Hume's vision the honest good disappeared and the delightful good was the only existing form of good, there was no need for a normative function of reason. Reason was only to show the means leading to pleasure and this therefore tied utilitarianism with eudaemonism. For this, Hume's position was strongly criticized by Immanuel Kant. Kant's opposition to utilitarianism and the eudaemonistic understanding of morality was coupled with his rejection of empiricism in the name of rationalism. Hume's moral sense was marked by the emotions, and Kant perceived in this a sign of egoism that distorted morality. He insisted, therefore, on the capacity of pure reason to issue a priori imperatives, imperatives of pure reason, free of any external influences and addressed to the pure will. These can be formulated according to the basic principle that behavior is to be such that it may become a rule for universal legislation. The attempt to liberate reason from any external dependencies coming from the emotions and the senses led Kant to an a priori formalism in ethics.

Wojtyła disapproved of such an avenue in ethics, because reason—following human experience, as Aquinas presents it—is understood to be a part of the human being, whereas Kant's pure reason was a purely artificial construct worked out uniquely for abstract philosophical analysis. Can the analysis of the practical reason, asked Wojtyła, be viewed only theoretically, divorced from the aspirations and actions of the human being?[12] Kant's reaction against utilitarian eudaemonism did not bring reason back into the mechanics of decision making as a normative force. Kant only declared the inherent independence of the practical reason from the emotions and from the causality of physical nature. This independence of pure practical reason is for Kant a synonym of morality. But, as Wojtyła noted, when reason is so elevated, it has no role in morality. If reason manages only to liberate itself from the determining influence of the emotions, it does not undertake the attempt to direct them. (It is good to remember that Aquinas saw the mutual cooperation of reason and the passions and not their absolute opposition.) Therefore, the interpretation of reason as a categorical imperative is, as Wojtyła noted, defensive against the physical nature and not directive. It denies the teleological dimension of all the faculties, leaving the reason in an abstract formal purity.[13] How different this vision is from that of Aquinas, who attributed to the reason the capacity of perceiving finalities and the truth about goodness and its inherent honesty, and the capacity to direct in a normative way human action—even though, in this, reason needs to exert effort so as to overcome the resistance that the subjective delightful good can offer. The entire energy of reason, however, as Wojtyła noted, is used not only in the overcoming of that resistance. Morality is built not on the resistance against the egoism of the delightful good, but on the foundation of the honest good, the splendor of which reason can in its truth perceive and to which it can, together with the will, freely adhere.

The next ethicist whom Wojtyła attentively studied was Max Scheler. Wojtyła noticed a basic difference between Scheler's understanding of the moral act and that of Aquinas. For Scheler, the emotional experience of moral value is primary. The emotional involvement of the individual in a world of values, established according to a certain hierarchy, is central. Therefore, it is not the "experience" of the truth about goodness, meaning the formulation of the norm, that would be highlighted, but only the "experience" of the value itself. The experience of the value in this system overshadows the experience of the truth about the good. For Scheler, an intuition of value is sufficient without placing its object under the light of truth. His emotionalism therefore has, as it were, swallowed the rich structure of the spiritual life of the human person capable of seeing the truth and willing it as such.[14] Wojtyła rejected this view as an emotionalist simplification that fails to focus on the viewing of the object in the light of truth, whereas only in this light is there a place for a norm. The insistence on the perception of the light of truth within the moral act allows for the formulation of the norm and therefore for a true ethics that could be a rule for life and not only a description of experiences.

In his 1956 to 57 lectures on norms and happiness, Wojtyła employed the phrase *splendor of reason* within his explanation of the heart of the moral act. In an essay published in 1959, he repeatedly used the phrase *the light of truth* in the same context, and in his book *Osoba i czyn* [*The Acting Person*], we find the phrase *the moment of truth*. These expressions, always highlighted by inverted commas, in some way prefigured the future encyclical of John Paul II on the principles of morality.

Theological Applications in the Papal Magisterium

The fundamental conviction of Karol Wojtyła that the acting subject is capable of discerning the true good and that precisely in this capacity lies the basic dignity and spiritual value of the mature human person was formulated within the context of philosophical ethics. As John Paul II, the Supreme Pontiff of the Church, Karol Wojtyła had to change the underlying key of his discourse. The papal magisterium is given within theology, a discourse that has the revealed truths about God and his love for humanity as its basic axiom. Therefore, the 1993 encyclical *Veritatis Splendor* (Regarding Certain Fundamental Questions of the Church's Moral Teaching) is centered on God's grace. The human question is, "Teacher, what good must I do?" The answer is a warning: "Do not be conformed to this world." To this the pope offers the fundamental motivation: "Lest the Cross of Christ be emptied of its power" (*Veritatis Splendor*, III, n. 85). The graces flowing from the cross of Christ are the basic gift that the Church has to offer humanity. The Church's moral teaching must be coordinated with this basic gift of grace, even though the capacity to perceive the *verum bonum*, which the spiritual faculties of reason and will by nature possess, is prone to error due to the distorting influence of mistaken philosophies and, even more so, due to the impact of an unformed and disordered affectivity. Since grace does not destroy but elevates human nature, this capacity to perceive the true good within the mechanics of moral decision making can only be made more lucid in the life of faith, and the adherence to it motivated from within by charity can only be strengthened, even though the effort of spiritual constancy in the face of a clearer understanding of challenges and responsibilities is not necessarily alleviated.

The encyclical *Veritatis Splendor* veers around the capacity of the spiritual faculties to perceive "the moment of truth" in all its splendor. It shows that moral law supplying a sapiential teaching is not an enemy of freedom but a necessary support for its spiritual growth. Conscience that is the act of the practical reason is not to be understood outside the realm of truth or within a skeptical, relativist approach to reason. Conscience is the inner window toward truth that supplies the light for the moral act. Although it is not creative in respect to the moral norm, which the reason has to formulate in the light of truth in its objectivity, it is certainly creative in respect to the act as it stimulates the courage to undertake acts of virtue. An understanding of the relationship of human endeavors toward God that would withdraw the realm of moral action from a reference to God and his grace—meaning that individual good and evil acts would have no significance on that relationship, and that just a vague fundamental option toward God with no bearing on individual and concrete acts would be sufficient—would ultimately deprive the world of human life and responsibility from any significance before God. This cannot be true, and therefore every human act has to be understood in its truth and richness, in which its moral object is viewed through the agency of the individual's reason.

Veritatis Splendor came as an answer to the debate that erupted at the Second Vatican Council and remained unanswered. A Christian view of morals is not centered on an objective moral order imposed from without by God and the Church. It is centered on divine grace, which from within heals the acting person, enabling the perception of the splendor of truth within the moral act and a generous adherence to it, and thereby empowering the mature person both to perceive the objective moral order within the splendor of truth of the moral act and the working out of a personal moral order within the sequence of human acts. That perception of the truth of the moral act is fundamentally personalist. In full accord with the oft-unnoticed personalism of St. Thomas Aquinas, the encyclical *Veritatis*

Splendor stresses that "the morality of the human act depends primarily and fundamentally on the 'object' rationally chosen by the deliberate will (...). In order to be able to grasp the object of an act that specifies that act morally, it is therefore necessary to place oneself *in the perspective of the acting person.*"[15] The italicized insistence on the interior perspective of the acting individual, which runs contrary to the expectations of the casuist mentality of previous centuries, is a direct fruit of the philosophical research of Karol Wojtyła. Moral action, experienced from within in all its richness and responsibility, and enhanced therein by supernatural grace, is the prime field of human maturity and human dignity: the insistence on this is the basic answer of the Church to the aspiration for personal liberty and for happiness that had animated the past century and certainly still animates the aspirations of the present.

The second major encyclical of John Paul II, *Fides et Ratio*, against the cultures of intellectual skepticism and its fruits—which are relativism, moral nihilism, and ultimately hedonism—defends the dignity of reason. Faith spurs reason on so that it would not stop short in its endeavors reaching to the fullness of truth. John Paul II trusted in the dignity of the human mind and clearly understood that faith does not impede the inquisitive search of the human mind, but on the contrary invites the mind to go further, to perceive the truth in all its splendor. We can only hope that this reflection on the influence of the grace of faith on the philosophizing mind will inspire in the Church a similar reflection on the influence of the grace of charity on the acting will and the felt affectivity, so that all the facets that contribute to the perception of and the adherence to the *verum bonum* will be illuminated.

BIOETHICS
From Vatican II to Pope John Paul II

PROF. GONZALO MIRANDA, LC
Bioethics faculty, Ateneo Pontificio Regina Apostolorum, Rome

Introduction

When John Paul II was elected pontiff, bioethics was only eight years old. Ethical reflections on the behavior of doctors, however, had already been going on for two thousand five hundred years, and the Catholic Church had been reflecting on these issues for two thousand years.

Throughout the years of his long pontificate, Pope John Paul II was concerned with a complex and changing cultural background. He accepted the challenges of the new opportunities and problems raised in the field of biomedicine and then studied in bioethics and offered specific contributions, chiefly, but not exclusively, for believers. In this, as in all areas of his magisterial teaching, he drew the sap of his ideas from the ancient roots of the Church's tradition. It was above all the treasure of the Second Vatican Ecumenical Council that inspired his teaching. In fact, in his first talk to the cardinals, the day after his election as pope, he strongly stressed, programmatically, his link with the Council: "Above all, we wish to insist upon the permanent importance of the Second Vatican Ecumenical Council, and for us that amounts to a formal commitment to implement it as it deserves."[1]

Just one month later, he mentioned for the first time a subject related to bioethics, praising the Union of Italian Catholic Lawyers because they had not given in "to the flattery and temptation to act with mistaken autonomy in proposing and defending the principles

83

of natural and Christian ethics governing the institution of marriage, and also in affirming the inviolability and the sacredness of the human life from conception, in usage and in law."[2] And it is significant that, in the same talk, there is explicit reference to two Council texts for proposing one of the central considerations of his reflection. He stated: "Society with its various laws is placed at the service of mankind; Christ founded the Church for the salvation of man"; and he quoted *Lumen Gentium*, n. 48, and *Gaudium et Spes*, n. 45.

From this first brief consideration right up to the end of his pontificate, the specific pronouncements of John Paul II on subjects related to bioethics and to respect for life in general were many, and they covered varied and complex issues.

In all this, the heritage of Vatican II has without doubt guided his reflections and his teaching. There are few direct references to the conciliar text itself, because subjects related to bioethics are not found often in them (they appear mostly in *Gaudium et Spes*, nos. 27 and 50–53). The underlying principles, however, especially on the foundations of the dignity of the human person, are profoundly rooted in the conciliar doctrine.

Here it is not possible, or perhaps even plausible, to attempt to gather together John Paul II's teachings on the specific subjects he tackled. It seems to me more interesting to attempt to trace some of the sources of his rich teaching in these areas.

The Importance of Bioethics

Throughout the years of his long pontificate, Pope John Paul II was not at all indifferent to the development of bioethics. The first time he expressly used the term *bioethics* was in 1986 in a talk to the academic body of the Catholic University of Lyon.[3] It is a term that he used in twenty-three of the documents of his pontificate. But, naturally, there are very many references made to these issues without referring explicitly to the term.

In the encyclical *Evangelium Vitae*, for example, he pointed to the birth and the development of bioethics as "positive signs" of the present culture,[4] and he invited bioethics centers and committees to give their own contribution for the propagating of a true culture of life.[5] In the apostolic exhortation *Christifideles Laici*, he exhorted the laity, who are committed for various reasons and at different levels in the fields of science and technology, such as in medical, social, legislative, and economic areas, to courageously accept the challenges presented by new problems in bioethics.[6] In the exhortation *Vita Consecrata*, among the tasks of consecrated persons he identified that they should "endeavor to make the practice of medicine more human, and increase their knowledge of bioethics at the service of the Gospel of life."[7]

The establishment in 1994 of the Pontifical Academy for Life was a clear sign of his preoccupation with this area. In the motu proprio *Vitae Mysterium*, with which he instituted the academy, he wrote that "all health-care workers are required to be properly trained in morals and the problems in bioethics."[8]

Our final example is his address directed to participants in the Third World Congress of Pro-life Movements, in which he stressed that "what is required is (…) formation in the important field of bioethics, most of all for health officials but also for every citizen."[9]

The Courage to Seek the Truth

Perhaps one of that pontificate's most important contributions in relation to bioethics was to have invited everyone to restore trust in human reason and to have the courage to seek the truth. John Paul II's call to philosophers in his encyclical *Fides et Ratio* is also perfectly applicable to bioethicists, "asking them to have the courage to recover, in the flow of an enduringly valid philosophical tradition, the range of authentic wisdom and truth—metaphysical truth included—which is proper to philosophical enquiry."[10]

In his speech to young people gathered in the Denver stadium (1993), the pope emphasized that restoring faith in the capacity to recognize truth was one of the most acute problems of modern culture and of today's youth.

Another important contribution without doubt came from his articulate and profound reflections on the foundations of morality in the encyclical *Veritatis Splendor*.[11] The only way to make sure that bioethics is not reduced to the "Permissions Office" denounced by

Neuhaus[12] is to get back the courage to seek the moral truth of our actions, even in the field of biomedicine, and even when our desires and our personal, economic, or political interests are involved.

Recovering the Ontological Dignity of the Human Person

The anthropological vision presented by John Paul II, beginning from the age-old tradition of Western Christianity, and renewed by his remarkable, intuitive capacity and by the strength drawn from his deep love of humanity, offers us a solid platform on which to build a bioethics that does not lead to discrimination against the weakest and instead promotes respect for every single human individual.

It seems quite significant that his first encyclical was dedicated to Christ as Redeemer of mankind, *Redemptor Hominis*. In that text he forcefully states that "man (…) is the primary and fundamental way for the Church."[13] Mankind should be—must be—the primary and fundamental way for bioethics too.

John Paul II often stressed that every single human being enjoyed a sublime dignity already from the point of view of his rational comprehension, but above all in the light of Christian revelation, as stated by the text of *Gaudium et Spes*, which he quoted in his own encyclical:

> "Human nature, by the very fact that it was assumed, not absorbed, in him, has been raised in us also to a dignity beyond compare. For, by his Incarnation, he, the son of God, *in a certain way united himself with each man*. He worked with human hands, he thought with a human mind. He acted with a human will, and with a human heart he loved. Born of the Virgin Mary, he has truly been made one of us, like us in all things except sin," he, the Redeemer of man.[14]

In his writings and talks, another very beautiful and profound statement from *Gaudium et Spes* appears: man as "the only creature whom God has loved for himself." The pope mentioned this phrase on at least seventeen separate occasions.

In Christian anthropology as told and retold by John Paul II, there is no place for a dualistic concept that degrades corporeality to a mere instrument and the human person to a mere phenomenon of consciousness. For Pope John Paul II, corporeality is not a marginal aspect; nor is it a weight from which one must detach oneself as quickly as possible. The Gospel of life affirms the indivisible union between person, life, and corporeality.[15] In this way, no attack against life or against the physical integrity of any human being can be justified.[16]

For the Christian, as the pope's words remind us, human life is always a "good."[17] And a similar statement indicates, basically, that the value of human life is intrinsic.

A Strong and Passionate Defense of Human Life

Finally, we can state that the encyclical already mentioned several times, *Evangelium Vitae*—an encyclical completely dedicated to the promotion of the culture of life against the advancing culture of death—was, is, and will be in future years a true map and a strong encouragement for all who wish to understand, love, and defend human life and the dignity of every individual human being without discrimination of any kind.

Here I will highlight, separately from his rich and eloquent arguments in favor of all aspects of human life, the three points in *Evangelium Vitae* at which John Paul II makes pronouncements with great solemnity and in a way similar to his pronouncements made *ex cathedra*:[18]

By the authority which Christ conferred upon Peter and his Successors, and in communion with the Bishops of the Catholic Church, I confirm that the direct and voluntary killing of an innocent human being is always gravely immoral. This doctrine, based upon that unwritten law which man, in the light of reason, finds in his own heart (cf. Rom 2:14–15), is reaffirmed by Sacred Scripture, transmitted by the Tradition of the Church and taught by the ordinary and universal Magisterium.[19]

By the authority which Christ conferred upon Peter and his Successors, in communion with the Bishops—who on various occasions have condemned abortion and who in the aforementioned consultation, albeit dispersed throughout the world, have shown unanimous agreement concerning this doctrine—I declare that direct abortion, that is, abortion willed as an end or as a means, always constitutes a grave moral disorder, since it is the deliberate killing of an innocent human being. This doctrine is based upon the natural law and upon the written Word of God, is transmitted by the Church's Tradition and taught by the ordinary and universal Magisterium.[20]

In harmony with the Magisterium of my Predecessors and in communion with the Bishops of the Catholic Church, I confirm that euthanasia is a grave violation of the law of God, since it is the deliberate and morally unacceptable killing of a human person. This doctrine is based upon the natural law and upon the written Word of God, is transmitted by the Church's Tradition and taught by the ordinary and universal Magisterium.[21]

Conclusion

John Paul II intervened strongly and clearly in the midst of the thought and debate surrounding bioethical issues throughout his pontificate, offering ideas, guidelines, and reference points that can truly be considered a treasure for the next generation.

WOMEN IN THE LIGHT OF MARY
From Vatican II to Pope John Paul II

DR. LAURA TORTORELLA

Pontifical Theology Faculty, St. Bonaventure

In his address to the general audience on January 12, 1966, Paul VI defined the Second Vatican Council "as a spring, from which a river gushes forth (…). The Council obliges us to look at the heritage which it has left for us and which is present and will last into the future." So, using Paul VI's image and applying it to the subject of the "woman" in Vatican II, we find this spring emerging from the documents, the inherited experience to be grasped and to bring to fruition.

The Council's Teaching about the Woman

The Second Vatican Council took place in a fully feminist climate. These were the years in which the emancipation of women was strongly linked to the sexual revolution, which not only claimed women's legal, political, and social equality with men but also, albeit with some variations from the feminist perspective, tried to "free" women from marriage, and therefore from family and from children through divorce and abortion.[1]

The Council, at that time, became an example of "openness" to the historical situation regarding women through their participation, for the first time in history, as auditors of the Council, but above all, through its teaching that promotes the participation of women in a range of activities: educational, family, civil, political, and ecclesial. We think of the Decree on the Apostolate of the Laity, *Apostolicam Actuositatem* (November 18, 1965), n. 9, which noted: "Since in our times women have an ever more active share in the whole life of society, it is very important that they participate more widely also in the various fields of the Church's apostolate."

We also think of the Council's message to humanity [given in Pope Paul VI's closing speech on December 8, 1965—ed.] in which, by defining women as "one half of the immense human family," the important equality between men and women was highlighted. We find in this message the promotion and encouragement of women: "The hour has come, (...) the hour in which women in society obtain an influence, a radiance, a power that has never before been achieved." Women are called to accomplish difficult tasks such as "helping humanity not to decay," "upholding home life," and "reconciling mankind with life." In addition, women are recognized in their roles as spouses and mothers of families and the "primary educators of mankind," and in their roles as consecrated virgins as "guardians of purity, selflessness, and piety."[2] This message spoke of "women put to the test," in difficulties clearly compared to the image of Mary at the cross: "You who have so often throughout history given men the strength to fight to the end, to witness to the point of martyrdom, help us once again to preserve the boldness of our grand schemes, together with patience and an awareness of our humble origins."[3] Another task that was entrusted to women in this message is to "help the spirit of this Council to penetrate institutions, schools, homes and daily life," to educate the world in the ways of peace "at this most crucial point in history."[4]

We can also find the Council's legacy on the subject of women in various passages from *Gaudium et Spes*, the Pastoral Constitution on the Church in the Modern World. For instance, n. 52 points out how motherhood and taking care of the family environment are not obstacles to the woman's search for human and social development, but instead, ways to find their creaturely and anthropological root in the sincere gift of self (see also n. 24). *Gaudium et Spes*, at n. 60, clarifies the call to Christians within the culture regarding women, because "it is now necessary for them to fully carry out their tasks according to their own nature. It is the duty of all to ensure that women's proper and much needed participation in cultural life be recognized and promoted."[5]

In light of the above it is possible to draw some conclusions about the Council and the development of the subject of the woman, which leads us to Paul VI's definition, with which we introduced this topic: the source.

The themes regarding the woman emerged as though from a spring, but the subject was not isolated and developed as a separate issue because, in this context, it was necessary to apply it to the whole of humanity, composed of men and women, and that, as we have seen, was already done. "The essentials [were] covered," as Rosemary Goldie, auditor at the Council, said. She also pointed out: "If, in looking at the final texts of the Council, we find silence on the subject of women, we know therefore that the silence is deliberate and significant; it has allowed us to apply to women all the openings provided by the Council for the participation of the laity in the life and mission of the Church."[6]

The Theme of the Woman in the Preparatory Documents

There is clear evidence for what Goldie states if we examine the documents of the preparatory committee and the many presentations of the Council Fathers. There are many references to the topic of women and they indicate great interest in studious reflection on the subject.[7] For example, in the preparatory committee's document on the lay apostolate, in *Schema Costitutionis* (n. 15), we find a brief text on women regarding individual apostolate, which is more developed than the final text of n. 9 of the decree.[8] In addition, in the same archive of the preparatory committee, we find documents that originate from external sources and that were distributed to all members on the issue of women,[9] which shows the attention of the committee itself to the role of women in society and in the Church.

We also find evidence of their interest in women's issues if we examine the work of some of the Council Fathers during the third phase of their undertaking. For example, the submission of Bishop Coderre, the bishop of Saint-Jean, Quebec, Canada, on the subject of the dignity of the human person, invited the Church to favor women's awareness of their identity, in order to allow their natural gifts to emerge, which are necessary for the realization of God's natural and supernatural plan. According to Bishop Coderre, the Church has the task above all of inviting Christians to help women to take their proper place in human society and in the Church, because God has created men and women equal and has given them a particular responsibility in the life of the Church.[10]

In this third stage of the work of the Council, the submission of Bishop Frotz, auxiliary bishop of Cologne (Germany), was also significant. He emphasized the changes taking place in the life of women that, in his view, were undervalued and that represented elements of extraordinary importance for the future evolution of society and the Church. According to Bishop Frotz, the Church must help women with adequate pastoral support to find the right balance between family and professional life. Above all, the Church must become the protector and promoter of the personal dignity of women, because the development or decline of society, the growth or loss of human culture, depends on the place that is given to women.[11]

Cardinal Browne, Bishop Quadri, Bishop Civardi, and Bishop Vial, in their respective presentations, again during the third period of the conciliar work, also spoke to the issue of recognizing the proper nature of women and their dignity.[12] Meanwhile, concerning the issue of women in the context of marriage and the family, several Fathers made pronouncements during the third phase, including Bishop Bednorz, who paused to reflect on working mothers, hoping to elicit from the Council an exhortation to the leaders of economic life that women be provided with professional occupations that allow them space for family life.[13]

In the fourth session of the work of the Council on *Gaudium et Spes*, the Pastoral Constitution on the Church in the Modern World, we also find various comments on the role of women in society and in the Church. Bishop Frotz intervened again on October 4, 1965, pointing out the need for women's contribution in cultural life,[14] while Bishop Franic spoke of women's right to education and culture.[15]

Women at the Council

As we have seen, the Second Vatican Council itself was the source with regard to the issues that were taken up concerning women, and itself was also a sign of visible change in that, for the first time, lay auditors participated; above all, religious and lay-women.

On September 14, 1964, at the solemn inauguration of the third session of the Council's work, Paul VI announced the Council's openness to women: "We are delighted to greet our beloved daughters in Christ, the 'women auditors' (...)." He goes on later to express the reason: "With a father's love we are moved toward all segments of the people of God, and how greatly every day we wish for Christian society to receive ever more abundantly the fruits of concord, mutual collaboration, good works and charity."[16]

Paul VI recognized that all of the women of the people of God have a privilege, which was expressed by Bishop Albino Luciani: "Only some men may say 'I am a bishop,' or 'I am a priest'; however, all women can turn to Christ and say to him: 'One of us has been your mother.'"[17] Therefore, Mary's motherhood is a point of communion with other women. Mary is woman, mother, role model, and perfect Christian, as defined by Paul VI in the apostolic exhortation *Marialis Cultus* (February 2, 1974) in the light of the teaching of Vatican II.

Women after Vatican II

After Vatican II, the Church's interest in the subject of women accelerated. In fact, in 1973, in response to a request of the 1971 assembly of the Synod of Bishops that called for a deep analysis of the theme of women for promoting a major contribution to community life, Paul VI drew up a study commission on women in society and in the Church.[18] The commission was charged with preparing the contribution of the Holy See to the 1975 United Nations Conference in Mexico, put forward on the occasion of the International Women's Year.[19] From that moment on, through the voice of the pope, the Pontifical Council for the Laity, and the secretary of state, the Church has always brought her teaching into all U.N. world conferences on the theme of women: Copenhagen (1980), Nairobi (1985), Beijing (1995).

Aware of social change and of the teaching of Vatican II, therefore, Paul VI welcomed the theme of women and dealt with it in order to find its theoretical foundations. This was a time of profound historical change and the pontiff saw the necessity of formation and education in order to allow women to take their rightful place in society and in the Church.

The Concept of Woman in John Paul II's Work

The woman and everything that revolves around her have always been elements in which Karol Wojtyła, then John Paul II, showed great interest.[20] The pope himself said: "Everything I have written on this theme in *Mulieris Dignitatem* I have felt since I was very young, and, in a certain sense, from infancy. Perhaps I was also influenced by the climate of the time in which I was brought up—it was a time of great respect and consideration for women, especially for women who were mothers."[21]

The teaching of John Paul II on women's issues has borne unprecedented and precious fruit.[22] He knew how to interpret the needs of the times, knew how to give tangible responses, and knew how to point out safe paths to follow.[23]

In the theological sphere, in order to study in depth the theme of the equal dignity of man and woman, he commented on the two versions of the creation of the man and the woman in the Book of Genesis and clarified the anthropomorphic biblical language.[24] John Paul II also highlighted occasions when Christ, by his behavior, demonstrated the equal dignity of man and woman: "'They were astonished that he was speaking with a woman' (John 4:27) because this behavior distinguished him from his contemporaries. Even the disciples of Jesus 'were astonished.'"[25]

In the philosophical sphere, the pope introduced "uni-dual" anthropology, where the person is considered in its unity and its duality. Beginning with experience, he showed that the other person is another "I" and that every "I" is defined as either male or female, with equal capacity and equal potentiality. What John Paul II proposes is an anthropology of unity in difference. This anthropology interprets man and woman as complements that can enrich each other, giving what is central to their being male or female. Thus, the relationship between man and woman is reciprocal and leads to a "unity of two," a *communio* of love that mirrors God's love for mankind.

God also has a *communio* of love that links the three Persons in one divine unity and makes the fact that *God is love* comprehensible. Creating man in his image gives God a likeness to his own *communio of love* that he can recreate by forming a union with another person: "In the 'unity of the two,' man and woman are called from the beginning not only to exist 'side by side' or 'together,' but they are also called *to exist mutually 'one for the other'*"[26] in order to discover together *the integral sense of their own humanity.*

John Paul II on Motherhood

Regarding women specifically, the pope showed how motherhood is an element that forcefully defines women and is a key stage for every man who comes into the world through a woman: "We were 'inside' our mother, but without being confused with her; we needed her body and her love, but were fully autonomous in our personal identity."[27] He examined motherhood in all its facets: biological and spiritual. Motherhood, on the one hand, expresses the

> specific potential of the female organism that with peculiar creativity conceives and generates the human being, with the help of the man. "'Knowledge' conditions procreation";[28]

> [yet on the other hand,] "['father' and] 'mother' in the world of persons are, so to speak, embodied ideals, models for others, and specifically for those whose personality must take shape and evolve within their spheres of influence. In this way, the order of nature goes no further than the biological facts which, within limits, are complete in themselves and final, but which in the world of persons acquire a new content of a kind which they cannot find in the natural order."[29]

In the cultural sphere, the pope's involvement in the question of women on the one hand indicated the importance of reflecting on the issue, and on the other, suggested the way to follow so that "we should rewrite history in a less unilateral way."[30]

The action of the woman has enormous importance; therefore, she must be free to operate in the family, but also in society, for the common good. He said:

> The commitment of the woman to all levels of family life also provides an essential contribution to the future of society and of the Church, which cannot be neglected without great damage to itself and to the woman herself, whether we take into account the conditions surrounding motherhood, or the intimacy that is necessary for children, the way in which babies and young people are brought up, the attentive and constant dialogue with them, or the care she brings to the many needs of a home, such that it remains welcoming, agreeable, comforting from an emotional point of view and provides cultural and religious formation. Who could deny that, in many cases, the stability and success of a family, its human and spiritual enrichment, are due very often to this maternal presence within the home.[31]

So it is only through the contribution of "feminine genius" that it is possible to build a "civilization of love."

John Paul II showed, in the ethical religious field, that women were given important roles even within the evangelical message:

> Many women accompanied Jesus and the apostles providing maternal support (cf. Luke 8:2–3); it is the "daughters of Jerusalem," who mark the cruel way of the cross with a note of pity (cf. Luke 23:27–30); women who share with His mother the appalling suffering of her Son at the foot of the cross (cf. John 19:23); women who have the privilege of being the first witnesses and announcers of the resurrection on Easter Sunday morning; women who, in the upper room, receive along with Mary, the gift of the Spirit (cf. Acts 1:14).[32]

In his teachings, the pope also stressed the innovations brought by the Council, as well as those of the magisterium, regarding the dignity of women. The Church has adorned herself all the more, thanks to the contribution and the presence of women "in the fields of evangelization, catechesis, liturgy, theology and, in general, the mission that the Church carries out in the world."[33]

John Paul II also gave a significant philosophical and theological contribution to bioethics, which as we know is interdisciplinary and uses knowledge from the experimental disciplines (medicine, chemistry, physics, genetics, biology, and so on), and also the non-experimental (philosophy, law, sociology, and so on). The pontiff intervened many times on the theme of women, for example, in preparation for the conference in Beijing in 1995, calling for reflection on aspects closely linked to bioethics: the transmission of life, the dignity of the woman, health policies, and more. In fact, John Paul II considered that a good outcome to the conference was impossible without a correct anthropological basis aimed at clarifying the dignity and aspirations of women.

The Dignity of Women and the Defense of Life

In recognizing the dignity of women, the pope grounded it in a universal human right, recalling the U.N. Charter, which for the believer stems from the truth about the creation of the human being in the image and likeness of God. Regarding women's aspirations, he drew attention to how often they suffer because their own fundamental dignity is not recognized.

The pope expected a response from the governments and organizations attending the Beijing Conference, an undertaking to promote and ensure legal guarantees regarding the dignity and the rights of women.

For John Paul II, it was impossible to respond to *the question of women* while ignoring the role of the woman in the family, since she is charged from the beginning with the responsibility for the protection of new life and then its care and harmonious upbringing.

At the Beijing Conference, he reflected on the trivialization of sexuality, which obscures morality and above all severely damages the dignity of women and their service to life. He called for the whole of society to pay attention to this moral degradation in relation to women and also to children, and not to settle for "easy" solutions that lead to promiscuity and to the sexual irresponsibility of abortion.

For Pope John Paul II, seeking just solutions for women meant more than anything protecting, loving, and respecting life, each and every life, and at every point of its existence.[34] John Paul II was a defender of life:

> It is necessary therefore to explicitly affirm human life from the first instant of conception in the heart of the mother; it is also necessary to defend this life when it is threatened in any way (even socially threatened); it is necessary and indispensable because, ultimately, we are dealing with *loyalty to humanity* itself, *loyalty to the dignity of mankind*. This dignity should be acknowledged from the beginning. If we destroy it in the womb of a woman, in the womb of a mother, then it will be difficult to defend it in so many other situations and areas of life and in human society. How can we speak of human rights when we violate this fundamental right? Many today expound on the dignity of man, but they do not hesitate to trample human beings when they are found weak and vulnerable, on the threshold of life. Is there not a hidden contradiction in all of this? We should never tire of repeating: the right to life is the fundamental right of every human being, *a right of the person, which should be asserted right from the beginning*.[35]

He was fighting against "what is euphemistically defined as 'interruption of pregnancy' (abortion). [This] cannot be evaluated with truly human categories other than those of the moral law, that is, of conscience."[36] He also identified one of the causes of abortion: the "contraceptive mentality" that has become so widespread that it provides the fertile ground for the abortionist mentality. In *Evangelium Vitae,* he stated that regardless of the intention of some to use contraceptives in order to avoid subsequent "temptations" to resort to abortion, such a mentality strengthens that very temptation. There is a very fine line between a "contraceptive mentality" and the "abortionist mentality."[37]

John Paul II, again in *Evangelium Vitae*, pointed out that the two mentalities, from a moral point of view, cannot be distinguished. Contraception damages the value and specificity of the conjugal act, separating the unitive moment from the procreative, and is opposed to the virtue of chastity. Through abortion, a human being is killed, which is opposed to the virtue of justice and to the commandment "Thou shalt not kill." It is clear that the moral depth of the two actions is different but, as the pope stated, they "are often closely connected, as fruits of the same tree (...). The life that could result from a sexual encounter thus becomes an enemy to be avoided at all costs, and abortion becomes the only possible decisive response to failed contraception."[38]

Through an analysis of John Paul II's talks on abortion, it is possible to identify some solutions that he traced throughout his pontificate: stressing the moral gravity of abortion; directing one's gaze toward the truth in order to *"call things by their proper names, without yielding to convenient compromises or to the temptation of self-deception"*;[39] forming the conscience on the twin principles of life and liberty in order to bring about a "cultural U-turn"; educating people in sexuality and the value of life, beginning from the ground up, that is, educating young people to use sexuality in the correct way; offering alternatives to mothers in difficulty.

On many different occasions John Paul II was criticized for his teachings, often viewed as limiting the freedom of women or too concerned with women's issues.[40] In reality, following the path of the life of the pope, his formation, and his experiences, it is possible to clarify how he believed profoundly in the gift of women and in their charism. By articulating his "uni-dual" anthropology, he made the creaturely root of the woman even clearer: her dignity, her role as a mother, her care, love, and communion. All these permit women to remain in the truth.

John Paul II spoke to all women and to all men about the role of women. He did so with a strength that came from his experiences and from his vision—his own life, and also his travels that brought him close to women and to their condition in every country in the world. He knew that the woman, guardian of life, still has a blank page on which to write the future of the human race. John Paul II placed great hope in women, such that, at the end of one of his talks, he stated: "There is no law laid down that says you must smile. But you can make a gift of your smile; you can be the leaven of kindness in the family."[41]

So, a woman's smile—a sign of love, welcome, and serenity—should become, following the pope's teaching, the symbol of a fierce battle against what he calls hard times.

Mary and Women

John Paul II pointed the way for women to reveal their own characteristics: Mary's eloquent teaching of how to overcome the differences between men and women; she is a reliable example for women of how to hold to the service of love, how to view man, be a help to him, and realize the plan of the Creator.

In the documents of Pope John Paul II directed toward women, Mary is often raised up as a living symbol of the "new" woman, a new principle, a new creature. Mary represents the "woman" just as the Creator wanted from the beginning:

> Mary is "the new beginning" of the *dignity and vocation of women,* of each and every woman (cf. St. Ambrose, De instit. Virg., V, 33: PL 16, 313) [...] and also *the discovery of her own feminine humanity.* He *"has done great things for me":* *this is the discovery of all the richness and personal resources of femininity,* all the eternal originality of the "woman," just as God wanted her to be, a person for her own sake, who discovers herself "by means of a sincere gift of self."[42]

Moreover, for Pope John Paul II, Mary is the heart of the salvific event. It is Mary, a woman, who says yes to man's salvation; her response of faith reflects her free will and therefore the participation of her feminine "I" in the Incarnation of Jesus Christ. However, as John Paul II explains, God does not accomplish anything that is not accepted *by the free will of the human "I."*

The pope reflected on another very important moment linked to Mary that gives rise to an element that is necessary for truly understanding the roots of women's dignity: service. In fact, in her dialogue with the angel, Mary, the one who is *full of grace*, expressed her own personal assent to the gift God wanted to give her, saying: "Behold, the handmaid of the Lord" (Luke 1:38). In this way she laid the foundations of a reign in which "to serve (...) means to rule" (*Lumen Gentium*, n. 36), because Christ himself is "the servant of the Lord" and demonstrated with his actions and his life the profound dignity and importance of service. Service, then, for the pope, acquired a very important meaning in that it represents the vocation and definitive union of every human being with God. Mary is the woman who, more than any other, has truly shown the validity and importance of service as an expression of that vocation present in every man who can fulfill himself by uniting himself to God as he was destined to when he was created.

Naturally, the fact that Mary gave birth to a son even though she had *not known man* can only be understood in the light of the Gospel. Her motherhood was not the fruit of matrimonial *knowledge* but the work of the Holy Spirit, and that son was a son who was given to her exclusively by God. This explains, therefore, how "Mary [...] maintained her virginal 'I have no husband' (Luke 1:34) and at the same time became a Mother."[43] In this way, Mary is at the pinnacle of the hierarchy of holiness and of giving. Mary embodies perfection because she is immaculate and without stain.

In the light of this, the pope defined the Church as *both* Marian [characterized by Mary's influence] and Petrine [characterized by apostolic succession—ed.]. It is Marian first, as Pope John Paul II stressed, because Mary, in all senses, preceded the apostles and possessed more.

THE FAMILY
The Place to Experience Communion

CARDINAL CARLO CAFFARRA
Archbishop of Bologna

In the philosophical reflection of Karol Wojtyła and in the teaching of John Paul II, the concept of "communion"—*communio personarum*—is the keystone to his entire discourse on marriage and the family.

Whether as the philosopher Wojtyła or as Pope John Paul II, he allowed the teaching of Vatican II to emerge. However, he also developed the teaching and created a completely original implementation of the Council: a great enrichment of the *Traditio Ecclesiae*.

In this presentation let us clarify, first of all, the concept of *communio personarum*. Second, we would like to show how this concept acts as the architectural principle of the doctrine on marriage and the family. Third, I wish to verify what capacity this doctrine has to interpret the situation in which we find marriage and the family, and therefore to direct the educational and pastoral action of the Church.

The Concept of *Communio Personarum*

In attempting to define the concept of *communio personarum*, the following axiom repeatedly emerges: "Only persons are capable of living 'in communion.'"[1]

A relationship is established between being a person and being in communion, by which on the one hand, communion is the proper and exclusive existential condition of the person, and on the other hand, the person's being, its ontological status, is revealed quite clearly in that communion. One could say that *communio* is the *ratio cognoscendi* [the truth] of the person and that the person is the *ratio essendi* of *communio*. This correlation or interdependency between the two variables—*communio* and person—pervades all of K. Wojtyła's philosophical thought and all of John Paul II's teaching. It also indicates the two main paths followed by his reflections: one being more properly anthropological in a general sense; and the other engaged in defining *communio personarum*.

His anthropological reflection aimed to answer this question: *Why is it that only a person can exist in communion?* The question returns to a classical subject in Western anthropological thought, considered from two different standpoints. The first standpoint is about the nature of mankind: Who or what is man? The second standpoint is about the social nature of the person: Is man naturally social?

But the point of departure in the thought of K. Wojtyła/John Paul II was not approached in exactly this way. He believed that the question about the nature of the person was already a question about his social nature, in that not to consider the person in connection with other people could be at most a procedural shortcut, to be used, with great theoretical vigilance, in order not to fall into anthropo-doxy instead of building a true anthropo-logy. In short, to start out by reducing the person to an individual—even if only methodologically—is theoretically and practically very dangerous. Furthermore, there is another point of originality in this same premise: the social and communal nature of the human person are not the same thing, just as society and communion are not the same thing.

The conciliar text that John Paul II quoted most frequently as the most perfect expression of the communal truth of the human person is this: "Man, the only creature on earth whom God willed for its own sake, cannot fully find himself except through a sincere gift of himself."[2] In the many comments that he made on this conciliar text, we find an outstanding example of his anthropology of communion. Here it is in a nutshell.

The paradoxicality of the human person comes from the fact that it has been "willed for itself" by God; it exists for itself. But at the same time it "cannot fully find itself except through a sincere gift of itself." The auto-teleological structure of the person realizes itself fully and paradoxically in the sincere gift that a person makes of itself. It loses itself, and can never find itself, if it refuses to give itself. Self-giving is the *logos* of the person: it is the final sense of its "being for itself."[3] Note that this is not an ethical reflection here on what the person ought to do, but rather a metaphysical reflection on the person's being.

Where does this communal aspect of the person come from? Or rather, why is it that the human person is itself and for itself only in giving itself?

The response is twofold. The theological response is that the human being "in the image and likeness of God" (cf. Gen 1:22) "does not find confirmation only in man's rational and free—that is, spiritual—nature (…). The likeness that man has to God he has because of the relationship that unites persons."[4] The human person's structure of communion ultimately finds its explanation in the mystery of the Trinity, the mystery that is the Unity of Three Persons in One Divinity.

There is also an anthropological response. It is the structure of the person that renders it capable of giving, capable of "the sincere gift of self." It is because they are persons that human beings are capable of giving themselves. In fact, it is only the being that is self-possessed and self-controlled that is capable of giving itself. No one can give what they do not possess. If, therefore, self-giving directly denotes a mode of action, this mode of action ultimately finds its explanation in the person's being: *operari sequitur esse*. As I have said, the gift of self reveals the person and is the *causa cognoscendi personam*; the person's being is *causa essendi* of the gift of self.

In reality, the conciliar affirmation, the guiding star of John Paul II's communion anthropology, speaks of the one who "fully finds himself" in giving himself; and, conversely, of the one who "loses himself" in refusing to give himself. It is at this point that we ask the ultimate radical question: *Why is it that the person's own structure, the framework of self-possession and self-mastery, is governed by giving (the man who finds himself) and not by refusing to give oneself, which also shows that the person possesses and dominates itself?*

It seems that the most articulate answer to that question was given in K. Wojtyła's essay "Participation or Alienation," published in 1977,[5] which enlarges on the last part of his main philosophical work *Person and Act*. It is not possible to follow the entire reflection through its various passages in this context. Once again, I will limit myself to essentials.

There are two points of departure. The first is that I live and act together with others, and those others are human beings who live and act with me. The second point is that the consciousness that I have of myself always includes every other person, whether near or far.

In acting alongside another, in cooperation, I understand that the other person is constituted in a way similar to me; I also understand that he too is an "I": that the other participates in humanity in the same way that I do, in a way that is appropriate to a person. A link is created that is not based on belonging to the same tribe, people, or so on. It is based on belonging to the same humanity as a person.

The essence of this other "I" reveals itself, not in separating itself from my own "I," but in participating in the same humanity. As K. Wojtyła said:

> The other's reality, however, does not come from categorical knowledge, humanity understood as man's conceptualized being, but comes about as the result of an even richer experience, in which a type of transference takes place of what we have been given as our own "I," outside of ourselves, to one of the other's, which in some way, appears as a different "I"—"another I"—"similar or close."[6]

The "I-others" relationship is not the application of an abstract concept of humanity to oneself and others. It is a relationship lived out concretely—unique and unrepeatable—in each encounter with another person.

However, to negate the other's "I," degrading it from *alius* (alter ego) to *aliud*, constitutes a grave impoverishment of oneself—as the Council calls it, a loss of oneself. The structure of self-possession and self-determination, which makes the person capable of giving itself, is betrayed, and so is impoverished and wasted if it does not fulfill itself through this experience of recognizing the other "I" as a person. The fundamental personalization of the relationship of every human being with every other human being is the only right way to fulfillment, to "fully find oneself." This certainly has various levels:

from *unicuique suum tribuere et alteri non laedere*, as Roman lawyers called it, to the gift of self that establishes *communio personarum*.

Finally, at this point, we can attempt a definition of *communio personarum*. It is a relationship made up of two or more persons who give themselves reciprocally and receive each other's "I." *Communio personarum* is an intelligible reality that has an intrinsic truth: it is the unity between persons who give themselves. It has an intrinsic goodness and preciousness: the good of communion, the common good that, in accordance with its nature, while it unites individual persons, ensures true goodness to each.

Marriage and Family as *Communio Personarum*

On a spiritual level, the highest form of *communio personarum* is *communio ecclesialis*. On the natural level, it is marriage and the family. Leaving aside the first of these, I would like to show how the aforesaid concept of *communio personarum* functions as the architectural principle of K. Wojtyła/John Paul II's doctrine of marriage and the family.

In 1975, quoting *Gaudium et Spes*, he wrote, "It seems that this doctrine of man, this theological anthropology, is presented as the core of this same human reality we call family." The twin anthropological statement—the person is for itself, the person finds itself in the gift of itself—is the truth, the *logos*, the core of the family. In fact, the same text continues: "From every point of view we must place man at the center of this reality. Every man takes his origin from it, as 'the creature that God willed for itself.' And each person within the family and through the family, seeks the realization of this same reality within himself that the aforementioned words express."[7]

All of John Paul II's teaching on marriage and the family is built on this personalist premise, whether in the doctrine itself or in ethics. We will see how, beginning from the reflection on marriage. We can find perhaps the most concise text in his apostolic letter *Gratissimam Sane*:

> In marriage man and woman are so firmly united as to become—to use the words of the Book of Genesis—"one

flesh" (Gen 2:24). Male and female in their physical constitution, the two human subjects, even though physically different, share equally in the capacity to live "in truth and love." This capacity, characteristic of the human being as a person, has at the same time both a spiritual and a bodily dimension. It is also through the body that man and woman are predisposed to form a "communion of persons" in marriage.[8]

We would like to highlight some parts of this conceptually rich text.

The capacity to "live in truth and in love" is equivalent to the capacity to "fully find oneself by giving oneself": a capacity that is equally present in both the man and the woman, since it is rooted in the ontological constitution of the person. But this capacity is imprinted not only on the spiritual dimension of the person, but also on its bodily dimension. This is a central statement in K. Wojtyła's anthropological thought and in the teaching of John Paul II. The body is able to experience and bring about the self-giving of the person. It is this capacity, which is both spiritual and corporeal, that defines the intimate identity of every man and every woman.

The proper nature of *communio personarum* that is instituted by marriage is precisely this: it is the person *as man* and the person *as woman* who give themselves. In this gift of self that goes to make up the *communio personarum* of marriage, the body forms an integral part as masculine or feminine. Masculinity and femininity, which determine the ability of the person to give itself, are the basis and the anthropological root of *communio coniugalis*.

What is revealed here is not just an anthropology of gift, but of the man-person and of the woman-person. The gift of self in which the person fully finds itself is at the root of conjugal communion; and the gift, in this case, is caused by a specific interpersonal love, spousal love. Conjugality is a particular relationship brought about by the gift of self, but which has not only a spiritual but also a physical dimension. It is established *from the body* and *in the body* because of and due to its masculinity or femininity. The proper mode of the spouses' reciprocal self-giving is dependent on their body and their sex, and at the same time on the union within this diversity and through this diversity.

The conjugal relationship certainly has many aspects and can be analyzed from various points of view. However, it seems that the type and the logic of the gift that constitutes *communio personarum* have key importance and are essential. This is so even when we consider the emergence of family from conjugal communion. The fact that the conjugal bond becomes the bond of fatherhood-motherhood—in other words, the fact of human procreation—must be understood in the light of the type of gift that it is and of *communio personarum*. I will now try to show this.

K. Wojtyła/John Paul II thought about the human race along two lines of reflection. The first was a profound examination of the intrinsic logic of conjugal communion in its twofold spiritual and corporeal dimension. This is laid out in a particularly thought-provoking way in a 1975 essay entitled "Fatherhood, Motherhood and *Communio Personarum*," and also in the apostolic letter *Gratissimam Sane*.[9] In the 1975 essay, the pope stated:

> *Communio personarum* in the conjugal relationship always requires the affirmation of being parents or the potential to be. Spouses must carry within the sexual act that conviction and availability that expresses itself in the consciousness that "I could become a father—I could become a mother." The rejection of this conviction and of this availability threatens the interpersonal relationship, that *communio personarum* expresses.[10]

I will limit myself to explaining the central point of this text: the free and conscious rejection of parenthood denies the *logos* of conjugality as *communio personarum*.

The second line of reflection is more directly related to the nature of the generative act, whether thought of actively or passively, as an act in which the logic of communion realizes itself.

The coming into existence of a new human being does not simply function as a means of perpetuating the human species. Human generation is not just the transmission of a biological life through a chain of individuals. Every human conception is a unique *quid* and a break with all repetitive continuity. This is true not just in the sense of genetic individuation, but by virtue of the fact that every human being is unique and irreplaceable. Each is precisely "willed for itself."

Parents cannot will a child "for itself": they must attribute to it its status and dignity as a person. The child enters into conjugal communion always as a person, and needs to be recognized and affirmed as such. Fatherhood, like motherhood, is a biological fact, but in *bios* the genealogy of the person is also true and the transmission of *humanum* (human nature). Bringing up children is a continual generation "until the person is formed."

But the gift of self happens not just from parent to child; it is also reciprocal. Since it enters immediately as a person, the child is capable of giving: its gift is simply to exist.

Here the anthropological axiom of Vatican II is fully realized. Precisely because the person of the man and the person of the woman as spouses exist for themselves, they find themselves fully in the gift of self and in the gift that they are to the child as spouses. The child in being a person that is "willed for itself" becomes itself—grows in humanity—through the gift that it makes of itself to its parents.

The conclusion, and here I close the second point of my reflection, which derives from this personal and communal vision of marriage and the family, is that the family is founded on marriage. It is irreplaceable, because the transmission of life to new persons can be an instance of *communio personarum*, and therefore of educating the person. The fact that the person is irreplaceable stems from its intimate communal nature. No other institution has a similar nature with equal intensity, and it is therefore unique in its ability to generate *humanum*. It is so unique that it has no equivalent in the true and proper sense.

Inside Postmodernism

As my final point, I would like to consider the situation in which marriage and the family are lived out in the postmodernist West. I will do so very schematically.

To avoid serious misunderstanding, I will say that I am not putting forward an argument based on statistics, nor on judgments about people. I am merely trying to identify the profile of a spiritual condition in which we find ourselves. What I am putting forward is the following thesis: the previous reflection on K. Wojtyła/John Paul II is an adequate interpretive and evaluative key of the current situation. This is the thesis that I will try to show here.

As I have already said, the reflections of K. Wojtyła and the teaching of John Paul II inseparably connect the doctrine of marriage and the family with the anthropological doctrine. Marriage and the family are rooted in the nature of the human person. This proposition is at the same time descriptive and prescriptive: according to the *logos* and *ethos* of marriage and the family. This revealed doctrine is confirmed by human experience and human experience leads to the revealed doctrine.

I believe that at the root of all the difficulties that the Christian standpoint faces today regarding marriage, there is a disconnect in and through postmodernity between marriage, family, and the nature of the human person. It is a disconnect that has led and is leading toward the complete "artificialization" of the family and marriage: they are thought of as mere social conventions, whose definitions are based exclusively on social consensus.

The disconnect I am speaking of is due to the denial of human nature as a universally valid truthful and evaluative criterion, which has now reached its ultimate goal. It affirms the relativity of every form that *humanum* can take, which makes it unthinkable that marriage and the family should be rooted in a *logos* and a stable and permanent *ethos*. The introduction of "homosexual marriage" into the legal systems reveals the depth of this challenge.

If there is one fact that emerges with crystal clarity from the thought of K. Wojtyła and the teaching of John Paul II, it is that the truth about marriage and the family and the truth about man have the same destiny: *simul stant—simul cadunt.*

It is not given to me to verify these statements on the fundamental articulation of the doctrine of marriage. I will restrict myself to one only: the trivialization of human sexual diversity. As human persons and as Christians, we cannot accept this. It is possibly the gravest anthropological error that poisons postmodernity. This trivialization means that masculinity and femininity are not the two modes of being of *humanum* as such, but are only forms of *humanum*

110

relative to the historical conditions that have given rise to them. The biological fact, therefore, which is obviously beyond discussion, has no reference outside of itself.

In the apostolic letter *Gratissimam Sane*, John Paul II wrote:

> Their constitution (being man or woman) and the specific dignity deriving from it, "from the beginning," defines the characteristics of humanity's common good in every dimension and area of life. Both the man and the woman make their own contribution to this common good, because of which, at the center of all human community, we find the attributes of communion and complementarity.[11]

To reject sexual individuation from our consciousness of truth and goodness changes the nature and the profile itself of the human common good. This becomes particularly evident in the conjugal relationship.

Drawing these reflections to a close, I believe I can state that the legacy left by John Paul II to thinkers and educators can be condensed into this statement: it is important to help man not to lose himself, not to forget the truth about himself, not to destroy the preciousness of himself. *Ne evacuetur Crux Christi*: that Christ's death not be in vain.

NOTES

The Reception of Vatican II in the Work and Documents of the Synod of Krakow (1972–79)

1. See George Weigel, *Witness to Hope: The Biography of John Paul II* (New York: Harper Perennial, 1999).
2. Karol Wojtyła, *Sources of Renewal* (San Francisco: Harper & Row, 1980), 5.
3. Ibid., 6.
4. *Przemówienie Księdza Metropolity w czasie ingresu*, "Notificationes e Curia Metropolitana Cracoviensi," 506 (1964), 86 (address of the metropolitan archbishop upon entry).
5. Wojtyła, 6–7.
6. Weigel, 264.

The Origins and Vocation of the Person

1. Cf. Laura Palazzani, *Il concetto di persona tra bioetica e diritto* [The concept of person between bioethics and rights] (Turin: Giappicchelli, 1996); Virgilio Melchiorre, *Corpo e persona* [Body and person] (Genova: Marietti, 1987); P. Kemp, *L'irremplaçable. Une éthique de la technologie* [The irreplaceable: An ethics of technology] (Paris: Cerf, 1997); C. Viafora, *Dire persona in bioetica* [Speaking of the person], in A. Pavan (ed.), *Dire persona. Luoghi critici e saggi di applicazione di un'idea* [Speaking of the person: Critical locations and essays on the application of an idea] (Bologna: Il Mulino, 2003), 147–73; R. Balduzzi, C. Cirotto, I. Sanna, *Le mani sull'uomo. Quali frontiere per la biotecnologia?* [Hands on man: What are the limits of biotechnology?] (Rome: Ave, 2005).
2. P. Singer, *Practical Ethics* (Cambridge University Press, 1999); H. T. Engelhardt, *The Foundations of Bioethics* (Oxford University Press, 1996). Cf. B. Cadoré, "L'argument de la dignité humaine en éthique

biomédicale" [The issue of human dignity in biomedical ethics], in *Le Supplement* 3 (1995): 73–98; A. Pessina, "Bioetica e antropologia. Il problema dello statuto ontologico dell'embrione umano" [Bioethics and anthropology: The problem of the ontological status of the human embryo], in *Vita e Pensiero* 79 (1996): 402–24, here 407; E. Schockenhoff, *Etica della vita. Un compendio teologico* [Ethics and life: A theological digest] (Brescia: Queriniana, 1997), 43.

3. Engelhardt, 126ff; Singer, 62 and 80.

4. Cf. P. Singer, *Animal Liberation* (New York: 1990).

5. Cf. J. Bailey, *Il postpensiero. La sfida del computer all'inteligenza umana* (Milan: Garzanti, 1998); in English, *Afterthought: The Computer Challenge to Human Intelligence* (New York: Basic Books, 1997). Also S. Williams, *Storia dell'inteligenza artificiale* (Milan: Garzanti, 2003); in English, *Arguing AI: The Battle for Twenty-First-Century Science* (New York: Random House, 2002).

6. Karl Barth, *Die kirchliche Dogmatik. Die Lehre vom Wort Gottes. Prolegomena zur kirchlichen Dogmatik*, I/1 (Zollikon-Zurich: Evangelischer Verlag, 1947), 386–87. Published in English as *Church Dogmatics*, tr. G. W. Bromley (Edinburgh: T&T Clark).

7. Cf. Karl Rahner, "The triune God as original and transcendent foundation of the history of salvation," in *Mysterium Salutis*, III (Brescia: Queriniana, 1969), 491: "As regards the 'anthropological turn' in modern times in the profane idea of person the subjective spiritual aspect became that which is thought in recto." Regarding the difficulties arising from the use of the term *person* in the Catholic tradition, cf. Joseph Ratzinger, "Il significato di persona nella teologia" [The meaning of person in theology], in *Dogma e predicazione* [Dogma and preaching] (Brescia: Queriniana, 1974), 173–89; F. Bourassa, "Personne et conscience en théologie trinitaire" [Person and consciousness in Trinitarian theology], *Gregorianum* 55 (1974): 471–93, 677–720; P. A. Sequeri, "La nozione di persona nella sistematica trinitaria" [The idea of person in the Trinitarian system], *Teologia* 10 (1985): 23–39; A. Milano, *Persona in teologia. Alle origini del significato di persona nel cristianesimo antico* [Person in theology: The origins of the meaning of person in early Christianity] (Rome: Dehoniane, 1996).

8. Cf. Boethius, *De persona Christi et duabus naturis*, 3 (PL 64:1343); St. Thomas Aquinas, *Summa Theologica*, I, q. 29, a.3, ad 2.

9. Richard of St. Victor, *De Trinitatae*, IV, 21–22 (PL 196:944–47): "persona est existens per se solum iuxta singularem quondam rationalis existentiae modum."

10. Ratzinger, "Il significato di persona nella teologia" [The significance of person in theology], 183. For the passage from the idea of substance to that of relation in defining the person, see *L'idea di persona* [The idea of person], V. Melchiorre, ed. (Milan: Vita e Pensiero, 1996).

11. Pontifical Council for Justice and Peace, *Compendium of the Social Doctrine of the Church*, nos. 108, 105.

12. For an up-to-date exposition of the bioethical reasoning in layman's terms, see *MicroMega* 2 (1997), which gathers together essays by C. A. Viano, M. Mori, E. Lecaldano, P. Flores D'Arcais, S. Rodota, and C. Flamigni.

13. E. Schockenhoff, *Etica della vita*, particularly the section "The Ethical Criterion of Selection: Personal Being and Human Being," 38–43, here 39–40.

14. Cf. Council of Europe, *Convention for the Protection of the Rights of Man and of the Dignity of the Human Being with regard to Biology and Medicine* (Strasbourg, 1995). For a broader historical context, cf. E. Berti, "Il concetto di persona nella storia del pensiero filosofico" [The concept of person in the history of philosophical thought], in *Persona e personalismo* [Person and personalism] (Padua: Gregorian, 1992), 41–74.

15. A good review of the different theories concerning the concept of person can be found in the work already cited by L. Palazzani, *Il concetto di persona tra bioetica e diritto* [The concept of person in bioethics and rights] (Turin: Giappichelli, 1996). The author reiterates that "the human being is person in virtue of its rational nature; they are not person because they possess certain attributes, because they perform certain functions or empirically verifiable actions" (239).

16. Schockenhoff, *Etica della vita*, 151.

17. For a clarification of these terms, see S. Leone, "L'embrione umano" [The human embryo], in *Rivista di Teologia morale* 46 (2005): 177–81; P. Cattorini, "Autonomia e libertà della scienza" [Autonomy and freedom of science], in *Rivista di Teologia morale* 46 (2005): 191–97. Cf. also P. Cattorini (ed.), *Scienza ed etica nella centralità dell'uomo* [Science and ethics in the centrality of man] (Milan: Franco Angeli, 1990).

18. Cf. R. Spaeman, *Persone. Sulla differenza tra "qualcosa" e "qualcuno"* (Rome-Bari: Laterza, 2005), 78; in English, *Persons: The Difference between "Someone" and "Something,"* trans. Oliver O'Donovan (Oxford: Oxford University Press, 2006).

19. The etiologist and primatologist Frans de Waal, in contrast to what we maintain, affirms that primates like the bonobo are able to understand the intentions, thoughts, and feelings of others and to share

them. He states, "It is not necessary to be men in order to be 'human.' All the large primates, chimpanzees, orangutans, gorillas and bonobos possess kindliness and the capacity to share emotional states. The roots of morality, a quality that is not uniquely human, can be traced in these cousins of ours." Cf. Frans B. M. de Waal, *Good Natured: The Origins of Right and Wrong in Humans and Other Animals* (Cambridge, MA: Harvard University Press, 1996); *Bonobo, The Forgotten Ape* (Berkeley: University of California Press, 1997).

20. J. Eccles, D. Robinson, *La meraviglia di essere uomo* (Rome: Armando, 1985), 41; in English, *The Wonder of Being Human* (Boston: Shambhala, 1985).

21. Cf. J. Splett, "Corpo, rapporto corpo-anima" [Body, the body-soul], in *Sacramentum-Mundi*, II (Brescia: Morcelliana, 1974), 634–42.

22. M. Luther, "Die Zirkularddisputation de veste nuptiali," in *Weimarer Ausgabe*, 39, I, 283, 1.

23. W. Joest, *Ontologie der Person bei Luther* (Gottingen: Vandenhoeck & Ruprecht, 1967), 36. Cf. also E. Schockenhoff, "Personsein und Menschenwürde bei Thomas von Aquin und Martin Luther," *Theologie un Philosophie* 65 (1990): 481–512, here 483–91.

24. A. Guggemberger, "Persona" [Person], in H. Fries (ed.), *Dizionario teologico* [Theological dictionary], II (Brescia: Queriniana, 1967), 648.

25. K. Rahner, *Spirito nel mondo* [Spirit in the world], M. Marassi and A. Zoerle, eds. (Milan: Vita e Pensiero, 1989).

26. R. Guardini, "La funzione della sensibilità nella conoscenza religiosa" [The function of sensitivity in religious consciousness], in *Scritti filosofici*, II (Milan: Fabbri, 1964), 137–90.

27. Ibid., 154.

28. Ibid., 164.

29. Guggemberger, 648. Cf. G. Novella, "Integrazione tra liturgia e spiritualità: problemi e proposte" [Integration between liturgy and spirituality: problems and proposals], in *Credere oggi* 98 (1997): 70–80: "The spiritual subject is the subject of flesh which, surrounded with God's love, lives in astonishment, suspended between the insignificance of its smallness and the wonder of its greatness," 71.

30. For a treatment of the problem of the mind's supremacy over the brain, see K. R. Popper, J. Eccles, *L'io e il suo cervello*, 3 vols. (Rome: Armando, 1981); in English, *The Self and Its Brain: An Argument for Interactionism* (Routledge, 1984). See also J. Eccles, D. Robinson, *La meraviglia di essere uomo* [The wonder of being human] (Rome: Armando, 1985).

116

31. Cf. the thesis of N. M. Ford, *Quando comincio io? Il concepimento nella storia, nella filosofia e nella scienza* [When do I begin? Conception of the human individual in history, philosophy, and science, 1988] (Milan: Baldini & Castoldi, 1997), and the confutation of his thesis in A. Serra, "Quando è iniziata la mia vita" [When my life begins], in *La Civiltá Cattolica* IV (1989): 575–85.

32. Schockenhoff, *Etica della vita*, 137, which maintains that the identification of person with individual is wrong. For man, being a person cannot coincide with being an individual due to the fact that he has always been a person, while the task of becoming an individual still lies before him. St. Albert the Great, *In Sententiarum*, I, d. 23, a. 3, in highlighting the theological origin of the concept of person, writes that the solution to the mystery of the person is to be found more in patria than in via: *dicimus sine praejudicio, quod istas questiones de persona, magis solvenda expectamus in patria, quam in via possimus.*

33. Cf. M. Nédoncelle, "Pròsopon et persona dans l'antiquité classique. Essai de bilan linguistique" [Prosopon and persona in classical antiquity: An essay of linguistic balance], in *Revue de Sciences Religieuses* 3–4 (1948): 227–300; C. Andresen, *Zur Entstehung und Geschichte des trinitarischen Personbegriffes, Zetschrift fur die Neutestamentliche Wissenschaft* 52 (1961): 1–39; C. J. Vogel, "The Concept of Personality in Greek and Christian Thought," in J. K. Ryan, ed., *Studies in Philosophy and the History of Philosophy*, II (Washington, DC: Catholic University of America Press, 1963), 20–60.

34. Guggemberger, 637: "This enfranchisement of the concept of person is a partial process within the larger historical process, through which, from the original theological thought of the West, arises the philosophy of life itself and a knowledge of its methods. The concept of person was secularized in the course of this process....Even when we do not acknowledge, or we in fact deny, the Christian origin of the concept of person, a philosophy of the person will still feed on this hidden or unacknowledged Christian root." Cf. also A. Milano, *Persona in teologia*; "La Trinità dei teologi e dei filosofi: l'intelligenza della persona in Dio" [The Trinity in philosophy and theology: Understanding the person in God], in A. Pavan and A. Milano, *Persona e personalismi* [Person and personalism] (Naples: Dehoniane, 1987), 1–282; O. Bucci, "La formazione del concetto di persona nel cristianesimo delle origini: 'avventura semantica' e itinerario storico" [The formation of concept of person in early Christianity: "semantic adventure" and its historical route], *Lateranum* n.s., 2 (1988): 383–450.

35. V. Melchiorre, "Per un'ermeneutica della persona" [An interpretation of the person], in Pavan and Milano, *Persona e personalismi*, 293.

36. W. Pannenberg, "Person," in *Die Religion in Geschichte und Gegenwart*, V. (Tubingen, 1964), 230–35. See also H. Ott, *Il Dio personale* [The personal God] (Casale Monferrato: Piemme, 1983); E. Jungel, *Dio, mistero del mondo. Per una fondazione della teologia del Crocifisso nella disputa fra teismo ed ateismo* [God, mystery of the world: A foundation of the theology of the crucifix in the dispute between theism and atheism] (Brescia: Queriniana, 1982), 72–80; D. Mongillo, "La condizione umana: struttura trinitaria e cristologica" [The human condition: the Trinitarian and Christological structure], in B. Lauret and F. Refoulé, eds., *Iniziazione alla practica della teologia* [Introduction to the Practice of Theology], III (Brescia: Queriniana, 1986), 608–14.

37. Thomas Aquinas, *In I Sententiarum*, 25, q. 1, to 2, c: "Respondeo dicendum, quod persona dicitur de Deo et creaturis, non univoco nec aequivoci, sed secundum analogiam, et quantum ad rem significatem per prius est in Deo quam in creaturis, sed quantum ad modum significandi est e converso, sicut est etiam de omnibus aliis nominibus quae de Deo et creaturis analogice dicuntur."

38. J. Galot, *The Person in Christ. A Theological Insight* (Vatican City: Pontifical Univ. Gregorian, 1981), 29, translated from the French by M. Angeline Bouchard.

39. Cf. I. Sanna, "Persona. Approccio storico-teologico" [Person: A historico-theological approach], in G. Cina, E. Locci, C. Rocchetta, and L. Sandrin, eds., *Dizionario di Teologia Pastorale Sanitaria* (Rome: Camilliane Press, 1997), 888–902.

40. Cf. C. Schütz and R. Sarach, "L'uomo come persona" [Man as person], in *Mysterium Salutis*, IV (Brescia: Queriniana, 1970), 318–19: "God did not create me, placing me outside of himself like a thing. No, he created me by calling me by name, by speaking. This name is at the same time a proclamation and a call to my person in love….Yes, everything about my being person is, on the one hand, a gift; and at the same time a commitment to respond to this loving and creative call. The most original relationship with this 'you,' or rather more accurately, the basis, the foundation, the beginning of the most profound relationship with this 'you,' is God's giving and creating call….God calls me his 'you,' until I can call him: 'you'."

41. Cf. G. von Rad, *Teologia dell'Antico Testamento* (reprint, Brescia: Paidea, 1972), I:163–69; in English, *Old Testament Theology* (Edinburgh:

Oliver and Boyd, 1962); R. Bultmann, *Credere e comprendere* [To believe and understand] (Brescia: Queriniana, 1977), 77–96; W. Kern, "La creazione quale presupposto dell'alleanza nell'Antico Testamento" [Creation as presupposition of alliance in the Old Testament], in *Mysterium Salutis*, IV, 59–77.

42. Cf. Plato, *Timaeus*, 29 b; 92 c. Even Aristotle does not speak of the soul as the unique form of the body, but as the world's universal reason, in which every individual man participates: Aristotle, *Metaphysics*, IV, 4; *De anima*, II, 1. Ancient philosophical thought speaks always of the essence of man and of his universal nature and thus does not take into account the uniqueness of each individual human creature. It succeeds in acknowledging the equality of all men but not the inalienable dignity of each single human being.

43. Cf. Mongillo, 609.

44. John Paul II, *Dives in Misericordia*, n. 1, *Enchiridion Vaticanum* VII, n. 860.

45. Cf. Mongillo, 609–10. In this sense we can understand H. Ott, who speaks of the "small reciprocity" between human beings depending on the "great reciprocity" between the divine persons. "If God determines our reality from all time without our knowledge, it means that he (and therefore also our own being before him) has shaped the reciprocity between human beings from all time, in which we exist as personal realities and in search of meaning. It is, therefore, in some measure, the small reciprocity as our normal condition that makes us encounter the great. Our minor reciprocity allows us to understand the nature of the major one, but also vice versa. This mutual illumination belongs to the revelatory experience of faith." H. Ott, *Il Dio personale* [The personal God], op. cit., 144–45.

46. Cf. *Gaudium et Spes*, n. 14. "Now, man is not wrong when he regards himself as superior to bodily concerns, and as more than a speck of nature or a nameless constituent of the city of man. For by his interior qualities he outstrips the whole sum of mere things. He plunges into the depths of reality whenever he enters into his own heart; God, Who probes the heart, awaits him there; there he discerns his proper destiny beneath the eyes of God. Thus, when he recognizes in himself a spiritual and immortal soul, he is not being mocked by a fantasy born only of physical or social influences, but is rather laying hold of the proper truth of the matter."

47. According to St. Thomas Aquinas, "Therefore, the intellectual nature is the only one that is required in the universe, for its own sake,

while all others are for its sake," *Contra Gentiles*, III, 112. *Gaudium et Spes* confirms that "for the beginning, the subject and the goal of all social institutions is and must be the human person which for its part and by its very nature stands completely in need of social life" (GS, 25). The so-called self-awareness of the person means that it can never be used as a means and therefore reduced to an object by any other created reality. To be used by another created reality alienates the person, while living for God corresponds to its ultimate goal, because God is more intimate to it than it is to itself: St. Augustine, *Confessions*, III, VI, 11.

48. Cf. E. Schockenhoff, *Etica della vita: Un compendio teologico* [Ethics of life: A theological digest], op. cit., 149.

49. Aboth de Rabbi Naathan, 31, in H. L. Strack, P. Billerbeck, *Kommentar zum Neuen Testament aus Talmud un Midrasch*, I (Munich: Beck, 1922), 750.

50. Cf. J. Ratzinger, "Il significato di persona nella teologia" [The meaning of person in theology], in idem, *Dogma e predicazione* [Dogma and preaching], op. cit., 183–84.

51. Cf. M. Bordoni, *Gesù di nazaret Signore e Cristo. Saggio di cristologia sistematica*, III: Il Cristo annunciato dalla Chiesa; in English, *Jesus of Nazareth, Lord and Christ: Essays in Systematic Christology*, III, Christ announced by the Church (Rome: Herder, 1986), 936.

52. J. Ratzinger, "Il significato di persona nella teologia" [The meaning of person in theology], op. cit., 184–85.

53. Cf. I. Sanna, *Chiamati per nome. Antropologia teologica* [Called by Name. Theological Anthropology], op. cit., 326–27. Cf. also L. Ladaria, "La unción de jesús y el don del Espíritu" [The anointing of Jesus and the gift of the spirit], *Gregorianum* 71 (1990): 547–71. According to Bonhoeffer, "Man's existence can be grasped, based on the truth and transferred into a new way of existing only in the person of Christ. And because the person of Jesus manifests itself in community, so man's existence can be grasped only in community. It is only by beginning with the person of Christ that every person can become so as a human being." D. Bonhoeffer, *Atto ed Essere. Filosofia trascendentale ed ontological nella teologia sistematica* [Act and being: Transcendental philosophy and ontology in systematic theology] (Brescia: Queriniana, 1985), 126. H. Ott points out, quite rightly, that the essence of the finite human person is the personality of the Triune God: H. Ott, *Il Dio personale* [The personal God], op. cit., 327. For P. Coda, by beginning with the event of Christ and his consequent widening of the Christological and pneumatological horizon, the human person reaches its full Trinitarian definition and takes on a constitutive Trinitarian essence:

P. Coda, "Personalismo Cristiano, crisi nichilista del soggetto e della socialità e intersoggettività trinitaria" [Christian personalism, the nihilist crisis of the individual, of community, and of Trinitarian relationships], in I. Sanna, *La teologia per l'unità d'Europa* (Bologna: EDB, 1991), 181–205, here 201.

54. Cf. M. Bordoni, "Il contributo della categoria teologica di persona" [The contribution of the theological category of person], in I. Sanna (ed.), *La teologia per l'unitá d'Europa*, op. cit., 59.

55. Following the Incarnation, the whole of humanity is assumed by Jesus, and the anthropological question is no longer, Who is the human being in Christ? The question is, Who is the human being in Jesus Christ and what will it become in Jesus Christ? See Mongillo, 612.

56. Bordoni, 60–61.

57. Cf. I. Zizioulas, *L'être ecclésial* [The ecclesial being] (Geneva: Labor et Fides, 1981), 42.

58. Ibid., 45–48.

59. Cf. Coda, "Personalismo Cristiano," 188–94.

60. Zizioulas, 48. On the role of Christology in the moral life of the believer and on how the call of God the Father in the Son builds man as a person, see the work of D. Capone, *L'uomo è persona in Cristo* [Man is person in Christ] (Bologna: EDB, 1973), and the essay of M. Doldi, "L'uomo è persona in Cristo. Nel pensiero di Domenico Capone" [Man is person in Christ in the thought of Domenico Capone], *Rassegna di Teologia* 39 (1998): 525–47.

61. Cf. Schockenhoff, *Etica della vita*, 479: "It is only when the Gospel of life finds echo in natural human reason, that its demands become clear to all."

62. Cf. I. Kant, "Fondazione della metafisica dei costume" [The groundwork of the metaphysics of morals], in *Scritti Morali*, ed. P. Chiodi (Turin: Utet, 1980), 97. "We can base the dignity of the human person on the fact that man is a naturally spiritual being, without immediately and directly referring to God, who remains the 'ultimate' foundation of that dignity, while man's dignity is its 'proximate' and 'immediate' foundation. However, this is dependent on condition that we have a spiritualistic conception of man, and not a purely materialistic, mechanistic or vitalistic one." "To Promote and Defend the Dignity of the Human Person," in the Editor's Preface, in *La Civiltá Cattolica* IV (1992): 231.

63. John Paul II, *Evangelium Vitae*, n. 2; cf. also 21.

64. J. L. Ruiz de la Peña, *Immagine di Dio. Antropologia teologica fondamentale* [The image of God: Fundamental theological anthropology]

(Rome: Borla, 1992), 184. The same consideration is noted in an editorial in the magazine of the Italian Jesuits: "It is not the case, historically, that the view of man as person was initiated and affirmed by Christianity and is owing to a reflection on the revelation of the Old and New Testament. In fact, it is precisely thanks to the discernment on creation of man as narrated in Genesis and on the redemption of man as enacted by Jesus Christ in his death and resurrection, that Christianity has grasped the highest dignity of man, created in the image of God, redeemed by Christ's blood and destined to live eternally with God as his son through his, not metaphorical but real, participation in his own divine nature." "To Promote and Defend the Dignity of the Human Person," *La Civiltá Cattolica* IV (1992): 231.

65. In order to get an idea of how this approach to the key points of the person is adequately defined, I quote two examples, from among many. J. Ratzinger writes that three modes of behavior belong to the essence of the personal being: subsistence (the conscious being-present-to-itself); existence (free openness to the world in the broadest sense of the phrase); and *communicatio* (self-giving and allowing oneself to give love only in the presence of personal reality): J. Auer and J. Ratzinger, *Il Mondo come creazione* [The world as creation] (Assisi: Cittadella, 1977), 380. U. Galeazzi writes that "from Christian thought, out of which still emerges a philosophy of the person, and from the doctors of the scholastic philosophy, the characteristics with which we can define the human person, are: rationality, finiteness, unity, singularity, inseity, perseity": U. Galeazzi, "Persona" [Person], in *Dizionario Teologico Interdisciplinare* [Interdisciplinary theological dictionary] (Turin: Marietti), II:707–8.

66. For a fuller explanation of these notes, see the aforementioned editorial "To Promote and Defend the Dignity of the Human Person," in *La Civiltá Cattolica* IV (1992): 228–29.

67. Cf. J. L. Ruiz de la Peña, *Immagine di Dio*, 183: "God is both the basis of man's personal being and at the same time the basis of I-thou relationships as interpersonal relationships. From this fact we can conclude with absolute truth that 'man is a finite version of God' (X. Zubiri, *El hombre y Dios* [Man and God] [Madrid: Alianza Editorial, 1967], 2) or that 'man is the diminutive of the divinity and the divinity is the superlative of man' (J. Pépin, *Idées grecques sur l'homme et sur Dieu* [Greek ideas of man and God] [Paris: Les Belles Lettres, 1971], 2)."

68. Thomas Aquinas, in III *Sententiarum*, q. 27, s. 1, a. 4, c: "res immateriales infinitatem habent quodammodo, quia sunt quodammodo

omnia, sive inquantum essentia rei immaterialis est vel potentia, sicut accidit in angelis et animabus."

69. Cf. Thomas Aquinus, *Summa Theologiae* I, q. 14, a. 2, ad 1; *De Veritate*, q. 2, a. 2, ad 2: "Reditio ad essentiam suam in libro de causis nihil aliud dicitur nisi subsistentia rei in seipsa. Formae enim in se non subsistentes, sunt super aliud effusae et nullatenus ad seipsas collectae; sed formae in se substentes ita ad res alias effunduntur, eas perficiendo, vel eis influendo, quod in seipsis per se manent; et secundum hunc modum Deus maxime as essentiam suam redit, quia omnibus providens, as per hoc in omnia quodammodo existentes et procedens, in seipso fixus et inmixtus ecteris permanent."

70. Cf. M. Buber, *Il principio dialogico e altri saggi* [The dialogical principle and other essays], A. Poma, ed. (San Paolo: Cinisello Balsamo, 1993), 59–83. For a study of dialogical philosophy, cf. B. Casper, *Das dialogische Denken. Eine Untersuchung der religions-philosophichen Bedeutung Franz Rosenzweigs, Ferdinand Ebners und Martin Buber* (Freiburg im Breisgau: Herder, 1967).

71. Cf. John Paul II, *Mulieris Dignitatem*, n. 7.

Verum Bonum in the
Moral Teaching of John Paul II

1. *Inter Mirifica*, n. 6.

2. *Liberté, que dis-tu de toi-même? Vatican II 1959–1965* (Saint-Maur: École Cathédrale; Parole et Silence, 1999), 446–63.

3. Karol Wojtyła, *Wykłady lubelskie* [The Lublin lectures] (Lublin: Wydawnictwo Towarzystwa Naukowego Katolickiego Uniwersytetu Lubelskiego, 1986), 73.

4. Karol Wojtyła, *O kierowniczej lub służebnej roli rozumu w etyce na tle poglądów św. Tomasza z Akwinu, Hume'a i Kanta* [On the directive and ancillary role of reason in ethics in the light of the views of St. Thomas Aquinas, Hume, and Kant], *Roczniki Filozoficzne* 6 (1958), in Karol Wojtyła, *Zagadnienie podmiotu moralności* [The question of the subject of morality] (Lublin: Wydawnictwo Towarzystwa Naukowego Katolickiego Uniwersytetu Lubelskiego, 1991), 216–19.

5. Karol Wojtyła, *Wykłady lubelskie*, 210.

6. Karol Wojtyła, *O metafizycznej i fenomenologicznej podstawie normy moralnej. Na podstawie koncepcji św. Tomasza z Akwinu i Maxa Schelera* [On the metaphysical and phenomenotogical foundation of the

moral norm: On the basis of the views of St. Thomas Aquinas and Max Scheler], *Roczniki Teologiczno-Kanoniczne* 9 (1959), in Karol Wojtyła, *Zagadnienie podmiotu moralności*, 240.

7. Wojtyła, *Wykłady lubelskie*, 69–70.

8. Karol Wojtyła, *Osoba i czyn* [The acting person] (Kraków: Polskie Towarzystwo Teologiczne, 1985), 169–71.

9. Karol Wojtyła, *O metafizycznej i fenomenologicznej podstawie normy moralnej*, 250.

10. *A Treatise of Human Nature* (Oxford, 1888), II, III, p. 415, quoted in Karol Wojtyła, *O kierowniczej lub służebnej roli rozumu w etyce*, 221.

11. Wojtyła, *O kierowniczej*, 224.

12. Ibid., 228.

13. Ibid.

14. Wojtyła, *O metafizycznej*, 251.

15. *Veritatis Splendor*, n. 78; italics are in the original.

Bioethics: From Vatican II to Pope John Paul II

1. John Paul II, radio message, October 17, 1978, in *Insegnamenti di Giovanni Paolo II*, I (1978), 14 [*Teachings of John Paul II*, I (1978)]. Later on, this text will be referred to as *Insegnamenti* [*Teachings*].

2. Talk to Catholic lawyers, November 25, 1978, in *Insegnamenti* [*Teachings*] I (1978): 209–14.

3. Address to the academic body of the university, Lyon, October 7, 1986, in *Insegnamenti* [*Teachings*] IX/2 (1986): 946–56.

4. The encyclical letter *Evangelium Vitae*, n. 27, in *Insegnamenti* [*Teachings*] XVIII/1 (1995): 761.

5. Ibid., n. 98, p. 832.

6. Post-synodal apostolic exhortation *Christifideles Laici*, n. 38, in *Insegnamenti* [*Teachings*] XI/4 (1988): 2134.

7. Post-synodal apostolic exhortation *Vita Consecrata*, n. 83, in *Insegnamenti* [*Teachings*] XIX/1 (1996): 812.

8. Motu proprio *Vitae Mysterium*, n. 3, in *Insegnamenti* [*Teachings*] XIX/1 (1996): 812.

9. Address to the Third World Congress of Pro-life Movements, October 3, 1995, n. 6, in *Insegnamenti* [*Teachings*] XVIII/2 (1995): 711.

10. Encyclical letter *Fides et Ratio*, n. 106, in *Insegnamenti* [*Teachings*] XXI/2 (1998): 453.

11. Cf. encyclical letter *Veritatis Splendor*, in *Insegnamenti* [*Teachings*] XVI/2 (1993): 275–375.

12. Cf. R. J. Neuhaus, "The Way They Were, The Way We Are," in A. L. Caplan (ed.), *When Medicine Went Mad: Bioethics and the Holocaust* (Totowa, NJ: Humana Press, 1992), 225.

13. Encyclical letter *Redemptor Hominis*, n. 14, in *Insegnamenti* [*Teachings*] II (1979): 630.

14. Ibid., n. 8, p. 620, quoting *Gaudium et Spes*, n. 22. Italics are in the original.

15. Cf. *Evangelium Vitae*, n. 81, in *Insegnamenti* [*Teachings*] XVIII/1 (1995): 816.

16. Cf. *Veritatis Splendor*, n. 50, in *Insegnamenti* [*Teachings*] XVI/2 (1993): 318.

17. Cf. *Evangelium Vitae*, n. 34, in *Insegnamenti* [*Teachings*] XVIII/1 (1995): 767.

18. On the theological interpretation that should be applied to these expressions, see K. J. Becker, "Competenza del Magistero e portata delle sue dichiarazioni" [Competence of the Teaching and the scope of its declarations], in E. Sgreccia and R. Lucas (eds.), *Commento interdisciplinare alla "Evangelium Vitae"* [Interdisciplinary Comments on *"Evangelium Vitae"*] (Vatican City: Libreria Editrice Vaticana, 1997), 299–314.

19. *Evangelium Vitae*, n. 57, in *Insegnamenti* [*Teachings*] XVIII/1 (1995): 791–92.

20. Ibid., n. 62, p. 797.

21. Ibid., n. 65, p. 801.

Women in the Light of Mary:
From Vatican II to Pope John Paul II

1. For an analysis of the principles of feminist interpretation, see L. Tortorella, *Fondamento, missione e possibile sconfitta della donna in Giovanni Paolo II* [Foundation, mission, and potential defeat of the woman in John Paul II], doctoral thesis, Pontificio Ateneo Regina Apostolorum, 2008, 105–11.

2. Cf. Second Vatican Council, *Messaggi del Concilio all'umanità* [The Council's message to humanity] (Bologna: Dehoniane Press, 1992), 240–41.

3. Ibid., 241.

4. Ibid.

5. Ibid.

6. R. Goldie, "Una donna al Concilio. Ricordi di una 'uditrice'" [A woman at the Council. Memories of an "auditor"], in *Rivista di Scienze Religiose*, Year II, no. 2/1988 (Molfetta: Pontificio Seminario Regionale Pius XI).

7. The documentation in question is the preparatory committee's document on the lay apostolate to be found in the historical archive of the Pontifical Council for the Laity.

8. *Schema Costitutionis De Apostolatu Laicorum, Pars Prima*, ch. 4, n. 25, *Schemata Costitutionum ed Decretorum*, fourth series (Vatican City: Typis Polyglottis Vaticanis, 1963), 62.

9. Cf. *La place de la femme dans la societè et dans l'Eglise* [The place of the woman in society and in the Church], Preparatory Committee, archive XX, 1–4; Investigation: *Vie de la femme dans l'Eglise* [The life of the woman in the Church], Preparatory Committee, archive XX, 8.

10. Cf. Msgr. G. Coderre, in *Acta Synodalia Sacrosancti Oecumenici Vaticani II, Periodus II, Pars V* (Vatican City: Typis Polyglottis Vaticanis, 1975), 728–29.

11. Cf. Msgr. A. Frotz, in *Acta Synodalia Sacrosancti Oecumenici Vaticani II, Periodus III, Pars VI* (Vatican City: Typis Polyglottis Vaticanis, 1975), 42–43.

12. Cf. Card. M. Browne, in *Acta, Periodus III, Pars V*, 437–38; Bishop S. Quadri, in *Acta, Periodus III, Pars VI*, 40; Bishop L. Civardi, in *Acta, Periodus III, Pars VII*, 214–15; Bishop M. Vial, in *Acta, Periodus III, Pars V*, 501–3.

13. Cf. Msgr. H. Bednorz, in *Acta, Periodus III, Pars VII*, 187–88.

14. Cf. Msgr. A. Frotz, in *Acta, Periodus IV, Pars III*, 251–52.

15. Cf. Msgr. A. Franic, in *Acta, Periodus IV, Pars II*, 732.

16. *Insegnamenti di Paolo VI* [*Teachings of Paul VI*], vol. II (Vatican City: Libreria Editrice Vaticana, 1964), 545; "Il saluto di Paolo VI agli uditori e alle uditrici" [Paul VI's greeting to the male and female auditors].

17. A. Luciani, *Un vescovo al Concilio: Lettere dal Vaticano II* [A bishop at the Council: Letters from Vatican II] (Rome: Città Nuova Editrice, 1983), 80.

18. This commission, presided over by Bishop Bartoletti, was active until 1976 and was composed of fifteen women and ten men of different cultures, nationalities, and competences.

19. The commission drew up a document on the woman in society

and in the Church, *La donna in una società a dimensioni mondiali: 1975* [The woman in a society with global dimensions, 1975], in *La Chiesa e l'anno internazionale della donna* [The Church and the international year of the woman] (Vatican City: Pontifical Council for the Laity, 1975). In an article published under the title "Mejores Prácticas" (Best practices), in *Conference Proceedings* (European Family Congress), March 9, 2007, R. Figueroa, head of the woman's sector of the Pontifical Council for the Laity, stated that this document "opens and responds to the challenges of new times which invite us to reconsider the reality of women, to a greater reciprocity and complementarity between men and women in the family, and a greater consciousness of the need for women's collaboration not only through motherhood but also together with man in building culture and in the pastoral work of the Church" (original text in Spanish).

20. John Paul II's catecheses dedicated to human love bear witness to his interest in this area: *Uomo e donna lo creò—catechesis sull'amore umano* [Man and woman he created them—catechesis on human love] (Rome: Città Nuova Editrice–Libreria Editrice, 1995); *Amare l'amore umano* [To love human love], ed. L. Melina and S. Grygiel (Siena: Cantagalli, 2007). On June 18, 1983, Karol Wojtyła wrote on human love: "To love means: to be near the person you love; to be near to love, with which I am loved. To love, then, means: to remember. To walk, in some way, with the image of the loved one in one's eyes and heart. It also means: to ponder this love, with which I am loved and to study more and more its divine and human greatness. To love means, ultimately: to stay awake" (D. Galati, "Un mistico chef a l'attore" [A mystic who is the actor], in *Tu Karol Wojtyła* [You, Karol Wojtyła], a quarterly international magazine, monograph, year I, no. 1 [September–December 1985]: 27).

21. John Paul II, *Crossing the Threshold of Hope* (London: Jonathan Cape / Random House, 1994), 216–17.

22. All the speeches of Pope John Paul II on the theme of the woman can be found on the CD-ROM, *Insegnamenti di Giovanni Paolo II* [*Teachings of John Paul II*] (Vatican City: Libreria Editrice Vaticana), entry: "woman."

23. On the concept of woman in John Paul II, cf. L. Tortorella, "Fondamento, missione e possibile sconfitta della donna in Giovanni Paolo II" [The foundation, mission, and challenge of the woman in John Paul II], doctoral thesis, op. cit., 171–76.

24. John Paul II, *Mulieris dignitatem* (Milano: Editrice Ancora, 1988).
25. Ibid., 34.

26. Ibid., 18.

27. John Paul II, "Dalla vocazione maternal deriva il singolare rapport della donna con la vita umana" [The unique relationship of the woman with human life derives from the mother's vocation], Sunday Angelus, July 16, 1995: *Insegnamenti* [*Teachings*] XVIII/2 (1995): 119.

28. John Paul II, "Il mistero della donna si rivela nella maternità" [The mystery of the woman reveals itself in motherhood], address of Wednesday, March 12, 1980: *Insegnamenti* [*Teachings*] III/1 (1980): 543.

29. K. Wojtyła, *Love and Responsibility* (San Francisco: Ignatius Press, 1993), 261.

30. John Paul II, Angelus address, August 13, 1995: *Insegnamenti* [*Teachings*] XVIII/2 (1995): 191–92.

31. John Paul II, "È un dovere capital riconoscere la dignità e I diritti della donna" [It is an important duty to recognize the dignity and rights of the woman], address to the Fifth International Congress on the Family, November 8, 1980: *Insegnamenti* [*Teachings*] III/2 (1980): 1086.

32. John Paul II, "Ribadita dal Concilio la dignità della donna" [The Council confirms the dignity of the woman], address of August 16, 1987: *Insegnamenti* [*Teachings*] X/3 (1987): 221.

33. Ibid.

34. Here there is explicit reference to nos. 5 and 87 of *Evangelium Vitae*.

35. John Paul II, homily in Piazza del Campo, September 14, 1980: *Insegnamenti* [*Teachings*] III/2 (1980): 631–32.

36. John Paul II, general audience, January 3, 1979: *Insegnamenti* [*Teachings*] II (1979): 12.

37. For this analysis by the pope, see the encyclical letter *Evangelium Vitae*, n. 13, in *Insegnamenti* [*Teachings*] XVIII/1 (1995): 745–46.

38. Ibid., 746.

39. Ibid., nos. 58, 793.

40. M. A. Macciocchi, "Le polemiche in Italia: ma Wojtyła crede nelle donne?" [Polemics in Italy: Does Wojtyła believe in women?], in *Le donne secondo Wojtyła* [Women according to Wojtyła] (Milan: Edizioni Paoline, 1992), 366–70; F. Alberoni, "Osservazioni sociologiche in margine alla 'Mulieris Dignitatem'" [Sociological observations in the margins of "Mulieris Dignitatem"], in M. A. Acciocchi, *Le donne secondo Wojtyła* [Women according to Wojtyła] (Milan: Edizioni Paoline, 1992), 281–89.

41. John Paul II, "La dignità della donna e della sua missione" [The dignity of the woman and her mission], Speech to API-COLF Association, April 29, 1979: *Insegnamenti [Teachings]* II/2 (1979): 1022.

42. John Paul II, *Mulieris Dignitatem*, n. 11.

43. Ibid., 46.

The Family:
The Place to Experience Communion

1. John Paul II, apostolic letter to families, *Gratissimam Sane* (February 2, 1994), n. 7, in *Enchiridion Vaticanum*, XIV, n. 177, p. 99.

2. Pastoral constitution *Gaudium et Spes* (December 7, 1965), 24, in *Enchiridion Vaticanum*, I, n. 1395, p. 815.

3. Cf. K. Wojtyła, *La famiglia come "communio personarum"* [The family as "communio personarum"], in *Metafisica della persona* [Metaphysics of the person] (Milan: Bompiani, 2003), 1467.

4. Ibid., 1466.

5. Cf. ibid., 1387–1407.

6. Ibid., 1391.

7. Ibid., 1464–65.

8. John Paul II, n. 8, in op. cit., n. 187, p. 105.

9. Ibid., n. 12, in op. cit., no. 212–24, pp. 125–35.

10. Cf. Wojtyła, *Metafisica della persona*, 1481–99, n.p.

11. *Gratissimam Sane*, n. 6, in op. cit., n. 176, s. 97.